INSIDE

T0035252

★★★★★★★★★★★★★★★★
YOUR MATCH ANNUAL 2024!
★★★★★★★★★★★★★★★★

PICK YOUR EURO DREAM TEAM 38

Hey, Jude!

JUDE BELLINGHAM 8

EURO 2024 GUIDE 14

WICKED WONDERKIDS 28

WSL RECORDS 66

THE TREBLE

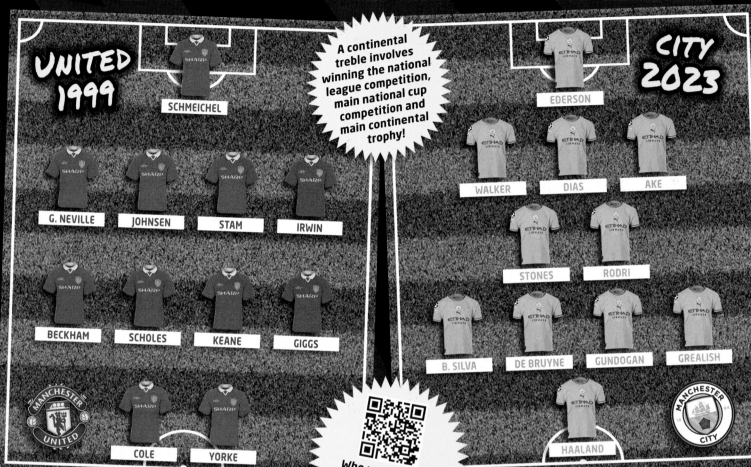

UNITED 1999

SCHMEICHEL

G. NEVILLE — JOHNSEN — STAM — IRWIN

BECKHAM — SCHOLES — KEANE — GIGGS

COLE — YORKE

CITY 2023

EDERSON

WALKER — DIAS — AKE

STONES — RODRI

B. SILVA — DE BRUYNE — GUNDOGAN — GREALISH

HAALAND

A continental treble involves winning the national league competition, main national cup competition and main continental trophy!

Who was the best treble-winning team? Scan the QR code to cast your vote!

MAN. UNITED

Man. United lost only four times in all competitions in 1999 but relied on some epic comebacks en route to the treble, notably in the FA Cup fourth round v arch-rivals Liverpool, the semi-finals of the Champions League v Juventus and, even more remarkably, their two stoppage-time goals in the CL final to defeat Bayern Munich 2-1!

MAN. CITY

Like The Red Devils, City didn't have it easy in 2022-23. They trailed Arsenal for the majority of the season in the Prem, before beating The Gunners twice in the run-in. A sweet success over United in the FA Cup final gave them bragging rights, before achieving their first European trophy win in 53 years by edging past Inter 1-0 in Istanbul in the CL final!

CONTINENTAL TREBLES!

The other men's teams to have won the UEFA continental treble...

CELTIC 1966-67

AJAX 1971-72

PSV 1987-88

BARCELONA 2008-09

KINGS!

IN GOAL!

The "Great Dane" Peter Schmeichel is one of the best goalkeepers of all time and lifted the 1999 Champions League trophy as captain in Roy Keane's absence! Ederson, meanwhile, is one of the best ball-playing goalies of the modern era and made one of the most important saves in City's history in the last minute in Istanbul!

IN THE MIDDLE!

United's crème de la crème midfield had David Beckham whipping crosses in from the right, Ryan Giggs dribbling past anybody on the left and Paul Scholes and Roy Keane bossing the centre with brains and brawn. City's six midfielders can out-pass the busiest press with each individual technically brilliant, while Kevin De Bruyne is already an all-time great!

AT THE BACK!

The United back line was a no-nonsense back four, filled with tough-tackling leaders whose main priority was to defend their goal. Pep Guardiola reverted to a back three in 2023, with Ruben Dias holding position, John Stones stepping into midfield, and the two full-backs tucking inside - similar to Ajax's Total Football system and Johan Cruyff's 3-4-3 formation!

OUR DEFENCE IS WAY MORE SOLID!

WE'D WALK INTO THE CITY XI!

YOU HIT 50+ GOALS COMBINED - I GOT THAT ALONE!

UP FRONT!

He didn't score in either final, but Erling Haaland finished as the CL and PL top scorer in 2022-23, breaking the record for the most goals in a single PL season! For United, Dwight Yorke and Andy Cole had a telepathic understanding, with Yorke finishing as joint-top PL scorer in 1998-99 and Cole bagging the goal that clinched them the title. Deadly duo!

THE GAFFERS!

Sir Alex Ferguson is the most successful manager in British football history, winning 13 Prem titles with United, ending their 26-year wait for a top-flight title in the inaugural PL season of 1992-93! City's Pep Guardiola is the fourth-most decorated manager of all time - behind Sir Alex, Jock Stein and Mircea Lucescu - and the only coach ever to win the continental treble on multiple occasions!

INTER
2009-10

BAYERN MUNICH
2012-13

BARCELONA
2014-15

BAYERN MUNICH
2019-20

HARRY KANE...
PREMIER LEAGUE LEGEND!

The Premier League said farewell to one of its all-time legends last summer in former Tottenham striker HARRY KANE! MATCH checks out some of his sickest PL stats...

213
His 213 Premier League goals are the most for a single club and sit him second in the all-time rankings behind Alan Shearer!

KANE
TOTTENHAM HOTSPUR
ALL-TIME RECORD GOALSCORER

47
He shared 47 goal contributions with Heung-min Son, making them the most prolific duo in Premier League history!

7
He won seven Premier League Player of the Month awards – an epic record he shares with Sergio Aguero. Hero!

LET'S GO, LIONESSES!

We're shouting out to The Lionesses for reaching the Women's World Cup final for the first time ever! Head to page 62 now to relive the awesome competition through our amazing WWC scrapbook!

POOCH PAL!

One of our favourite moments of 2023 was when a random dog appeared at Samuel Umtiti's reveal as a new Lille player! The pooch wasn't going to let the former Barcelona CB be the centre of attention!

SAY WHAT?

Chelsea and Australia striker Sam Kerr revealed the secret superstition which helps her succeed on a matchday – she eats a plain pasta sandwich before every match! Are you for real?

26

He holds the record for the most games scored in during a single PL season, shared with former Man. United striker Andy Cole!

39

His 39 Prem strikes in 2017 is a record for the most goals in single calendar year!

9

He also holds the record for the most consecutive seasons to score at least 15 goals - nine seasons, from 2014 to 2023!

INTERNATIONAL FOOTY IN 2024!

Check out the international football to watch in 2024...

ASIAN CUP

12 January - 10 February

Just over a year after hosting the World Cup, Qatar are hosting the postponed 2023 Asian Cup, using six of the eight stadiums from the WC!

AFRICA CUP OF NATIONS

13 January - 11 February

Hosted by Ivory Coast, the AFCON was also postponed from 2023. Reigning champions Senegal are hoping to hold on to their crown!

EUROPEAN CHAMPIONSHIP

14 June - 14 July

All European eyes will be on Germany as they host Euro 2024! Turn to page 14 to read our ultimate guide on the tournament!

COPA AMERICA

20 June - 14 July

A special edition of the Copa America features teams from CONMEBOL and CONCACAF and will take place across the United States!

OLYMPICS

24 July - 10 August

Seven stadiums in France will host the men and women's Olympics football tournos, with the men's version restricted to Under-23 players!

WHAT'S NEXT?

Check out some of Harry Kane's top targets in Germany!

1
The Three Lions captain can become the first-ever Englishman to win the Bundesliga Golden Boot! How many goals will he end up with in 2023-24?

3
Kane can become just the third Englishman to win the Bundesliga title - after Kevin Keegan (with Hamburg) and Owen Hargreaves (with Bayern)!

3
He could join Hargreaves and Steve McManaman as only the third Englishman to win the Champions League with a foreign club, as well!

DON'T MISS!

Turn to page 78 now to discover the Premier League players with the most all-time goal involvements!

50 RECORD BREAKERS!

At the start of 2023, Barcelona Femeni became the first professional team in men's or women's football to win 50 matches in a row in their national top-flight league!

INSIDE VIEW!

Ever wondered what it's like to play a professional footy match? This Youri Tielemans bodycam, from their pre-season clash with Newcastle, gives you a pretty good idea!

NICE NICKNAME!

Tottenham goalkeeper *Guglielmo Vicario* is also known as "Venom", like Spiderman's arch-nemesis from Marvel's comics! Apparently it comes from his anger on the pitch when he concedes a goal!

Hey, Jude!

I'LL GO ON TO BECOME A MADRID LEGEND!

LAURIE CUNNINGHAM
1979–1984

The left-winger signed from West Brom for close to £1 million, bagged a brace on his Real Madrid debut and went on to win a La Liga and Copa del Rey double in his first season! However, one of his most memorable moments in a Madrid shirt came in 1980, when he was applauded by rival Barcelona supporters at the Nou Camp during a Man of the Match display!

REAL RATING! 10/10

NOT A BAD RECORD, MATCH!

REAL RATING! 5/10

MICHAEL OWEN
2004-2005

Owen joined England team-mate David Beckham at Real Madrid after moving from Liverpool for £8 million, but things didn't work out for the nippy net-buster. He spent most of the season warming the subs' bench for Brazil duo Ronaldo and Robinho and, despite finishing 2004-05 with the club's best minutes-to-goal ratio, was shipped back to England in 2005 for double the money!

HAALAND'S HOBBY!

THE REAL GOAT!

ERLING HAALAND loves playing video games but, in an interview with Sky, he said it's "too embarrassing" to admit what he plays. We reckon it must be Goat Simulator the way he's been performing this year!

DAYOT PAVAROTTI?

MIC CHECK - ONE, TWO!

Bayern Munich defender **DAYOT UPAMECANO** has been working with an opera singer in 2023 as he gets sore throats after shouting during games and wants to improve his vocal chords!

3.5BN

According to Inter Miami co-owner David Beckham, Lionel Messi's presentation as a new player had 3.5 billion views! That's almost half the world's population!

BELLINGHAM'S BUCKET LIST!

- ☒ WIN LA LIGA! ☑
- ☒ WIN THE COPA DEL REY! ☑
- ☒ WIN THE CHAMPIONS LEAGUE! ☑
- ☒ REACH 100 CLUB APPEARANCES! ☑
- ☒ SCORE A GOAL AGAINST BARCELONA! ☑
- ☒ WIN REAL MADRID'S PLAYER OF THE YEAR! ☑

DAVID BECKHAM
2003-2007

Becks arrived in the Spanish capital as a proper hero after rejecting a move to Real's rivals Barcelona that same summer! Even though he joined during the club's Galactico period - playing alongside the likes of Zinedine Zidane, Ronaldo and Luis Figo - he only lifted one La Liga title and a Spanish Super Cup in his time there, but was a fans' favourite for his mega work-rate and commitment!

REAL RATING! 7/10

JONATHAN WOODGATE
2004-2007

The former England centre-back was a surprise signing in Spain due to his previous injury problems and spent his entire first season in Madrid on the sidelines! He finally made his Real debut in September 2005 but it was a total disaster - he scored an own goal and got sent off! Woodgate played just nine league games for Los Blancos and was voted their worst signing of the 21st century by the club's supporters!

TAXI FOR WOODY!

REAL RATING! 1/10

WILL YOU WIN THIS CUP, JUDE?

STEVE McMANAMAN
1999-2003

"Macca" joined Real Madrid from Liverpool on a free transfer and spent four really successful years in Spain, winning two La Liga titles and two Champions League medals! His Man of the Match performance and goal in the 2000 CL final also saw him become the first English player ever to win Europe's premier club competition with a foreign team!

REAL RATING! 9/10

THEY SHOOT, THEY SCORE...
...THEY DON'T LOSE!

In 2022-23, Arsenal's *Gabriel Jesus* became the player with the most Premier League games scored in without losing! Here's the top ten...

#	Player	GAMES	WINS	DRAWS
1	GABRIEL JESUS	55	50	5
2	JAMES MILNER	54	43	11
3	DARIUS VASSELL	46	36	10
4	DIOGO JOTA	36	30	6
5	SALOMON KALOU	32	29	3
6	OYVIND LEONHARDSEN	28	21	7
7	PEDRO	27	26	1
8	GABRIEL MARTINELLI	24	20	4
9=	ANTONIO VALENCIA	23	22	1
9=	GEORGINIO WIJNALDUM	23	19	4

MLS MELTDOWN!

Talking about MLS, their official Twitter account welcomed Sergio Busquets to the league by using a photo of...ex-Spain and Real Madrid defender Alvaro Arbeloa. Total fail!

RONALDINHO JR.!

Over 31 million people have watched this cool viral clip of Ronaldinho's son **JOAO MENDES** making his Under-19 debut for Barcelona in 2023! It might not be the most amazing clip you'll ever see, but it's a moment of history if he can follow in his father's footsteps!

DID YOU KNOW?

LUTON TOWN FOOTBALL CLUB
EST 1885

By winning the 2023 Championship play-off final v Coventry, Luton became the 51st club to feature in the Premier League! Can you remember who number 50 was?

P.R.O.J.E.C.T WREXHAM!

MATCH takes a look at how WREXHAM have gone from the non-league shadows to global football stardom almost overnight!

CELEBRITY OWNERS!

Once upon a time, two Hollywood actors applied to buy a non-league Welsh club with a history of financial problems. We're talking about Rob McElhenney and Ryan Reynolds, of course, who kick-started Wrexham's fairy tale by completing their takeover of the club in February 2021. An initial £2 million was put into the club's bank account, before a media tornado helped sweep the National League outfit towards the global limelight!

> THAT ONE'S FOR YOU, RED DRAGONS FANS!

STAR SIGNINGS!

Wrexham's newfound stardom has made them an attractive club for potential players, highlighted by ex-Premier League goalkeeper Ben Foster coming out of retirement to finish the 2022-23 season with them! Former Wales forward Hal Robson-Kanu also offered to play for them for free, while there was even gossip linking Gareth Bale with a shock move to the club before the rumours got shut down!

SOCIAL MEDIA BOOM!

By the time the 2022-23 campaign had ended, Wrexham had 517,000 followers on Twitter, 879,000 on Instagram, 238,000 on Facebook and 1.3 million on TikTok! New fans have begun to appear all over the world with some even travelling from as far as Canada to attend matches! More matchday revenue and extra cash from sponsorship deals means more money in the bank!

A HISTORY OF WREXHAM AFC!

1864
It was formed by members of Wrexham Cricket Club, making it the third-oldest professional team in the world. Wowzers!

1957

A club record 34,445 fans packed into the Racecourse Ground to watch Wrexham v Man. United in the FA Cup!

1976

They reached the last eight of the European Cup Winners' Cup, the equivalent of today's Europa Conference League!

FAMOUS FOOTY OWNERS!

MATCH reveals other celebs to have owned or invested in footy clubs...

ELTON JOHN
WATFORD

The world-famous musician is a lifelong Hornets fan and became club owner in 1976! They rose from the fourth division to the top flight during his tenure!

DELIA SMITH
NORWICH

The food at The Canaries' canteen must be goated with celebrity chef Delia Smith as their owner! She famously gave a rousing half-time speech back in 2005!

WILL FERRELL
LOS ANGELES FC

American comedy actor Ferrell – from Christmas film Elf – became co-owner of MLS outfit Los Angeles FC in 2016 and can often be seen at the stadium!

NATALIE PORTMAN
ANGEL CITY FC

Oscar-winning actress Portman founded Angel City FC in 2020, who entered the NWSL two years later! Tennis icon Serena Williams has also invested in the club!

LEBRON JAMES
LIVERPOOL

The four-time NBA winner bought two per cent of Liverpool in 2011, and The Reds regularly release LFC x LeBron clothing collections!

PROMOTION PARTY!

Of course, just having tons of followers on social media doesn't guarantee success, so we're shouting out to gaffer Phil Parkinson and his side for bagging over 100 points in the National League last season to seal promotion to the EFL – and end 15 years of non-league pain! Their objective now is to get promoted from League Two as quickly as possible!

WREXHAM AFC 1864

> HOLLYWOOD COULDN'T HAVE SCRIPTED IT ANY BETTER!

WELCOME TO WREXHAM

DISNEY DOCUMENTARY!

The club's profile has clearly been raised by Disney+ documentary Welcome to Wrexham, which centres on the Hollywood pair's attempts to revive the team and follows their side's performance under the new ownership. Thankfully for McElhenney and Reynolds, it has a far happier ending than Sunderland 'Til I Die, which is what inspired them to create the series in the first place!

1992
Fourth division Wrexham beat reigning English champions Arsenal in one of the FA Cup's greatest-ever giant killings!

2008
HEREFORD 2-0 WREXHAM
WREXHAM ARE RELEGATED
Wrexham entered administration in 2004 and eventually dropped out of the Football League in 2008!

2011
Fans raised £127,000 in one day to save the club from oblivion, before it was taken over by the Wrexham Supporters' Trust!

2021
Owners Ryan Reynolds and Rob McElhenney officially completed the purchase of the club in February 2021!

2023
Wrexham returned to the Football League in style after finishing top of the National League table with 111 points!

WIN PRIZES!

RIG 300 PRO GAMING HEADSET!

Thanks to our great mates at Nacon, you could win an epic multi-platform RIG 300 PRO gaming headset!
We've got eight of the top-quality headsets to give away. Get in there!

8 PRIZES!

The awesome multi-platform headset comes in ultra-classy black or white colourways!

Oversized earcups provide extreme comfort, while the cushioned headband reduces pressure so you can game for hours!

The cool performance microphone flips up for storage or travel, while inline mute and volume controls are included with max lock position!

CLOSING DATE: JAN. 31 2024

RIG | ⊙ nacon

For more information on this incredible gaming headset and more cool gaming accessories, head over to nacongaming.com and follow @Nacon

HOW TO ENTER! ▶  **VISIT...SHOP.KELSEY.CO.UK/WIN**

Then click on the competition image and enter your details. Full T&Cs are available online.

PORTUGAL

FERNANDES

FACTFILE!

DOB: 08/09/94
Club: Man. United
Country: Portugal
Position: Att. midfielder
Top Skill: Vision

Footy Fact! Bruno Fernandes has represented his country at the World Cup, European Championship, UEFA Nations League and the Olympics. What a total legend!

10 THINGS YOU NEED TO KNOW ABOUT...
EURO 2024

The European Championship kicks off in Germany in the summer of 2024 – here's everything you need to know!

1 THE HOSTS

This will be the fourth major men's tournament in Germany after the World Cups in 1974 and 2006, plus the Euros in 1988. The hosts have a decent record on home soil, winning in '74 and reaching the semis of the other two comps, so the pressure will be on to deliver again here!

2 PLAY-OFF DRAMA

For only the third time there will be 24 teams at the Euros, but we won't know the final line-up until March 2024 – that's when the play-offs take place to decide the last three sides heading to Germany! There's sure to be tons of excitement – we can't wait!

3 DUTCH DELIGHT

Germany might have a good record on home soil, but the Netherlands' record in their neighbours' back yard isn't bad either! The Dutch reached their first-ever World Cup final back in 1974 and lifted their only major trophy in Munich in 1988! Could they bag some more luck this time?

4 EPIC STADIUMS

Because they've got so much experience of hosting big tournaments, Germany has tons of quality grounds – more than they need for this tournament, in fact! They don't just look cool, they're also known for their amazing atmospheres - turn over to find out more!

Allianz Arena

5 TIGHT TURNAROUND

The last Euros were delayed for a year by COVID, while the 2022 World Cup took place in winter instead of summer, which means that this will be the third major international tournament in three years for many of the sides. Hopefully the players won't be too tired!

6 ENGLAND'S AGONY

England lost on penalties at Wembley in the final of Euro 2020, which means they now hold the record of qualifying for the most European Championships without winning it! Euro 2024 will be The Three Lions' 11th appearance at the Euros – can they finally land the trophy?

7 WICKED WONDERKIDS

New superstars are always born during the Euros! Back at the last tournament the likes of Pedri, Bukayo Saka and Jamal Musiala introduced themselves to Europe, while Poland's Kacper Kozlowski became the youngest player in European Championship history! Who will make a name for themselves this time?

8 THE HOLDERS

The last few years have been absolutely crazy for Italy! Although they won Euro 2020 and got to the Nations League finals later in 2021, they've also failed to qualify for the last two World Cups! What will be the next twist in the tale?

9 FRENCH FAVOURITES

The 2022 World Cup finalists are currently rated as favourites to win the trophy in Germany, and we can see why! Their captain, Kylian Mbappe, is one of the best players on the planet and they've got world-class depth in every position! Can anyone stop them?

10 RONALDO'S RECORDS

This will surely be Cristiano Ronaldo's last-ever tournament! If CR7 does go to Germany, he'll be the first player to play at six different Euros – a record that will probably never be beaten – while he also already owns the all-time record for most goals and games too!

STADIUM GUIDE!

MATCH reveals the sick stadiums that'll be used in Germany...

MERKUR SPIEL-ARENA

City: Dusseldorf ★ **Capacity:** 51,031

The fact that Germany has four clubs in the second division with 50,000+ stadiums tells you how much of a footy-mad country it is! Fortuna Dusseldorf's home was built ahead of the 2006 World Cup but wasn't chosen as a venue, so the locals are buzzing for the Euros!

MERCEDES-BENZ ARENA

City: Stuttgart ★ **Capacity:** 54,906

Germany have picked this ground for their second game, and they'll be hoping for a repeat of the last time they played there in a tournament. At the 2006 World Cup, they won 3-1 against a Portugal team starring a young Cristiano Ronaldo!

SIGNAL IDUNA PARK

City: Dortmund ★ **Capacity:** 65,849

All eyes (and ears!) will be on the famous Yellow Wall at the southern end of Dortmund's quality ground. With space for over 24,000 fans to stand, it's the biggest terrace for standing supporters in Europe, and helps create one of the fiercest atmospheres!

RED BULL ARENA

City: Leipzig ★ **Capacity:** 42,959

The smallest ground that will be used at this tournament is also the newest. The Red Bull Arena – or "Zentralstadion", as it was called before RB Leipzig moved in – was built in 2004, but you can still see the old ground from the outside. Cool!

VELTINS-ARENA

City: Gelsenkirchen ★ **Capacity:** 54,740

One of the newer stadiums at the 2006 World Cup, England have bad memories of this ground - Portugal beat them on penalties in the last eight! Schalke's home has got some great features, like a retractable roof and four huge screens that hang above the pitch!

VOLKSPARKSTADION

City: Hamburg ★ **Capacity:** 52,245

Hamburg play in the second tier of German football these days, but they're still one of the biggest clubs in the country with a wicked stadium! Older Fulham supporters will remember it - this is where they played in the final of the Europa League in 2010!

OLYMPIASTADION

City: Berlin ★ **Capacity:** 74,461

The massive ground in Germany's capital city is no stranger to massive finals. Barcelona won the 2015 Champions League at this ground and Italy won the 2006 World Cup here - when France captain Zinedine Zidane was famously sent off for a headbutt in his last-ever game!

DEUTSCHE BANK PARK

City: Frankfurt **Capacity:** 54,697

The Deutsche Bank Park - or Waldstadion, as Eintracht Frankfurt fans call it - is almost 100 years old and has been used at tons of major events! It's seen games at the 1974 and 2006 World Cups, the 2011 Women's World Cup and Euro '88 - plus loads more!

ALLIANZ ARENA

City: Munich ★ **Capacity:** 70,076

German champions Bayern used to share this ground, but their local rivals 1860 Munich moved out in 2017. It's not quite as big as the Olympiastadion, but it's more modern and has a quality atmosphere - that's why Germany are kicking off the tournament here!

RHEIN ENERGIE STADION

City: Cologne ★ **Capacity:** 49,827

This was the venue of the 2020 Europa League final when Sevilla beat Inter 3-2 but, due to COVID, there were no fans in the ground. It'll be totally different at the Euros, though - the supporters are packed in and close to the pitch, so the noise will be deafening!

24 BEST EUROS MOMENTS

1 Panenka Pen!

You've probably seen loads of players take a Panenka penalty, but the original was back in the final of Euro '76. Czech legend Antonin Panenka won the trophy for his country with a genius pen that's been copied ever since!

2 Pearce's Penalty Passion!

England defender Stuart Pearce missed a crucial penalty at the 1990 World Cup, but he made absolutely no mistake from the spot against Spain six years later as The Three Lions won a shootout for the first time!

3 Vintage Zlatan!

Zlatan Ibrahimovic scored six goals at the Euros, and almost all of them were absolute worldies! The best was his ridiculous backheel volley against Italy back in 2004 – we're still trying to figure out how he managed to get the ball in the net!

4 Sick Schick!

Absolutely nobody saw this unbelievable goal coming – especially not David Marshall! The Scotland goalkeeper was well off his line when Czech Republic striker Patrik Schick picked up the ball on the halfway line, before firing it into the net from way out. Worldie!

5 Great Danes Shock Europe!

Denmark only qualified for Euro '92 after Yugoslavia were kicked out, yet they ended up going all the way and winning the trophy! They built their shock success on a rock-solid defence and plenty of luck – they only won two of their five games over 90 minutes!

6 Hal Spins Out Belgium!

Euro 2016 was a seriously special summer for Wales as they made it all the way to the semi-finals! Hal Robson-Kanu helped them get there with a brilliant Cruyff Turn and sick finish against Belgium in the quarter-finals!

7 Trezeguet's Golden Goal!

With seconds left on the clock, Italy were set to win the final of Euro 2000, only for France to score a dramatic late equaliser through sub Sylvain Wiltord! Then, in extra-time, fellow Les Bleus sub David Trezeguet thumped home a stunning Golden Goal to win the trophy!

9 Wayne The Wonderkid!

Wayne Rooney was still only a teenager when he played for England at Euro 2004 but he absolutely bossed the tournament, scoring four goals - starting with a brilliant brace against Switzerland in the first game!

11 Greek Gods!

Nobody expected Greece to even get out of their group at Euro 2004, but they overcame hosts Portugal and pipped Spain on goals scored before winning 1-0 in all of their knockout games to lift the trophy in Lisbon!

8 Icelandic Heroes!

For a country with a population the size of Stoke, it was a miracle Iceland even qualified for the Euros - yet they made it all the way to the quarters in 2016, holding Portugal to a draw and knocking England out in the last 16!

10 Spain Destroy Italy!

No European team had ever won three major international tournaments in a row until Spain won two Euros either side of the 2010 World Cup! They sealed it in style too, hammering Italy 4-0 in the final of Euro 2012. Legends!

12 Gazza's Wondergoal!

One of the best and most famous goals in the history of English football happened at Euro '96! Paul Gascoigne got on the end of a long ball, chipped it over the head of a Scotland defender, and drilled home a volley!

13 Tails Never Fails!

After Italy and the USSR finished goalless after extra-time in their 1968 semi-final, the Italians went though by winning a coin toss. Madness!

14 Platini Masterclass!

At Euro '84, France's Michel Platini scored in every game on the way to the trophy - including two hat-tricks - and ended with nine goals in total!

15 Sturridge Sinks Wales!

When England took on Wales at Euro 2016, it was heading for a tense 1-1 draw - until Daniel Sturridge scrambled home a last-gasp winner!

16 Irish Eyes Are Smiling!

If you wanna see some absolute limbs, check out Robbie Brady's dramatic late winner v Italy at Euro 2016! It took the Republic of Ireland into the knockout stages for the first time ever!

17 Suker Punch!

Peter Schmeichel was one of the best keepers in the world at Euro '96, but he was embarrassed by Croatia striker Davor Suker's cheeky chip!

18 Van Basten Volley!

An unbelievable volley from an impossible angle, Marco van Basten's Euro '88-winning strike for the Netherlands is one of the greatest goals ever!

19 Scandinavian Surprise!

The only possible result that would have seen both Sweden and Denmark qualify from Group C - at Italy's expense - at Euro 2004 was a 2-2 draw... and that's exactly what happened!

20 Zizou Magic!

Zinedine Zidane showed why he was regarded as one of the best players ever with an all-time great display v Portugal in the Euro 2000 semis!

21 Ricardo's Penalty Heroics!

Ricardo didn't just make a vital save in Portugal's Euro 2004 penalty-shootout win v England - he did it after taking off his gloves, then stepped up to slam home the winning pen. Clutch!

22 Swiss Roll Over French!

World champions France were 3-1 up against Switzerland with just ten minutes to go in the last 16 at Euro 2020. Yet the Swiss scored two late goals before dumping them out on penalties!

23 De Hammer!

Remember Frank de Boer? Before he flopped as manager of Crystal Palace, he was a world-class Dutch CB with a lethal left foot - as he showed at Euro 2000 with a thumping free-kick v France!

24 England's First Final!

England were convinced the Euro 2020 trophy had their name on it! They beat rivals Germany in the last 16, thrashed Ukraine in the quarters, knocked out Denmark in the semis and went 1-0 up in the final - yet lost on penalties to Italy!

MATCH'S...
Crystal Ball!
2024!

Retirement Home!

After agreeing a new 12-month contract with Roy Hodgson for the 2023-24 season, Crystal Palace offer to convert one of the treatment rooms at Selhurst Park into a three-bedroom bungalow for the 76-year-old boss – that way, even if things go pear-shaped, he still has a home at the south London side's base!

Germany Gaffe!

In an attempt to improve their terrible recent record at major international tournaments, Euro 2024 hosts Germany decide to recall their entire Euro '96-winning squad! The plan badly backfires when half the team gets injured in the warm-up for their opening group-stage game – and they end up finishing bottom of the group!

We've looked into our crystal ball to predict what LOL stuff could happen in 2024!

I'm A Celebrity!

Becoming bored with his spell in Saudi Arabia, Cristiano Ronaldo makes a desperate attempt to get back into the European limelight by agreeing to appear on the 2024 version of I'm A Celebrity...Get Me Out Of Here! He makes it into the final after a gruelling first week of being nominated for every challenge, but misses out on the crown...to I'm A Celeb legend Harry Redknapp!

Mystery Musicians!

Clearly inspired by 2023's mystery Premier League rapper DIDE, a new masked boy band appear on the scene under the name "Wonderkids"! Their first smash hit "Banana Bread" breaks sales records and peaks in the UK charts at No.1, until a leaked memo reveals their true identities...managers Neil Warnock, Claudio Ranieri, Marcelo Bielsa and Sam Allardyce!

Scouting Secrets!

The Premier League's traditional big six decide to team up and hire a world-famous private investigator to discover the secret behind Brighton's epic scouting system! After five months undercover at the club, the hidden agent reveals that instead of some fancy formula or algorithm, Seagulls scouts actually just use a free online "random footy name generator". Busted!

Fundraiser Fail!

In order to raise cash for a shiny new stadium to rival Everton's Bramley-Moore Dock, Liverpool manager Jurgen Klopp offers to perform a 24-hour TikTok LIVE concert alongside Reds fans to be aired around the world! The "Klopp 'n Kop Rock around the TikTok Clock" raises £4 million in its first hour before the stream drops due to too many viewers!

Miracle Merch!

In a brainy bid to boost merchandising sales, Chelsea release a new range of flexible fashionable toy models of their players! The bouncing "Super Stretchy Sanchez Doll" sells out within the first hour of going on sale, while the "Hurling Whirling Sterling Doll", which spins as it travels through the air, is Christmas 2024's number one best seller!

SWEDEN

BLACKSTENIUS

VINICIUS JUNIOR

THE SAMBA SUPERSTAR!

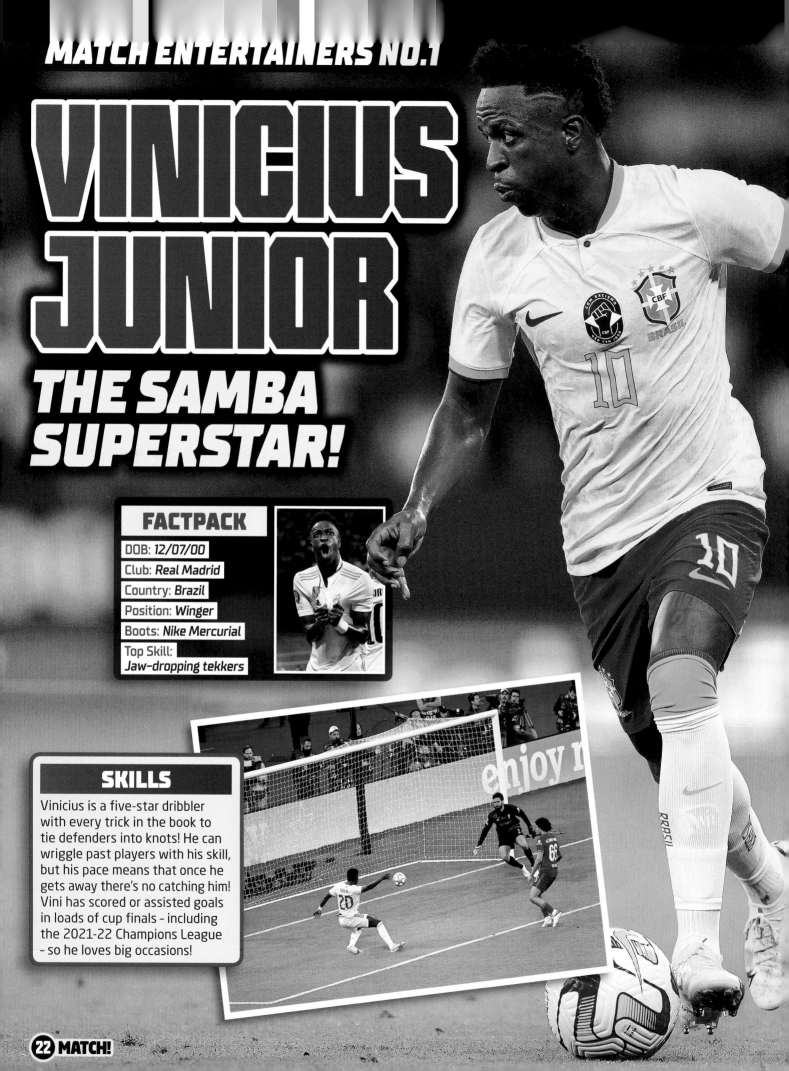

FACTPACK

DOB: 12/07/00
Club: Real Madrid
Country: Brazil
Position: Winger
Boots: Nike Mercurial
Top Skill: Jaw-dropping tekkers

SKILLS

Vinicius is a five-star dribbler with every trick in the book to tie defenders into knots! He can wriggle past players with his skill, but his pace means that once he gets away there's no catching him! Vini has scored or assisted goals in loads of cup finals - including the 2021-22 Champions League - so he loves big occasions!

STORY

No country on the planet produces ballers like Brazil does, and Vinicius Junior is the latest in a very long line of stars that includes legends such as Neymar, Ronaldinho, R9 Ronaldo and Pele! Real Madrid knew he was a star from the age of 16, as they paid over £40m to sign him in 2018, and over the last couple of years he's gone from being a promising youngster to the main man in attack for both Real and Brazil!

SHOW REEL!

Take a look at some of Vinicius Jr.'s best moments...

Flamengo v Emelec, 2018

Stunning solo goals like this one was one of the main reasons why Real Madrid were so keen to snap up the Brazilian prodigy!

Man. City v Real Madrid, 2022

Vinicius Junior left his Brazil team-mate Fernandinho choking on dust, then raced through to score in the CL semi-finals!

STYLE

Like a lot of Brazilian players, Vini learned his game playing futsal. The small-sided game is played with a small, heavy ball and is all about skill and technique – and Vini brings his best tricks out onto the football pitch! He's capable of doing things that most players wouldn't even think of, but he backs it all up by scoring and creating goals too!

Real Madrid v Liverpool, 2022

It doesn't get any bigger at club level than scoring the winning goal in the UEFA Champions League final!

HE PLAYS LIKE...

Neymar

Cutting in from the left wing with his speed and tricks, Vinicius is like a younger version of Neymar! Brazil's record scorer is the current owner of their famous No.10 shirt, but Vini is going to be asking for it very soon!

Brazil v South Korea, 2022

Vini Jr. bagged his first-ever World Cup goal with a smooth finish, then put in a pinpoint cross for Brazil's fourth goal!

WHAT'S IN STORE FOR 2024?

At the start of 2023-24, Madrid made a huge statement by handing Vini Jr. the No.7 shirt, which had previously been worn by the club's last two record scorers – Cristiano Ronaldo and Raul! He's going to lead the Spanish giants' new-look front line, and will do the same for Brazil when they head to the USA in the summer for the Copa America!

Real Madrid v Villarreal, 2023

As well as scoring a classy solo goal, Vini showed his flair by controlling one long-range pass with his back. Mind-boggling!

BIG MATCH QUIZ!

How many of these Premier League teasers can you get right?

FLIP FOR IT!

You've got a 50/50 chance of getting these mind-boggling brain teasers right. Tick the answer you think is correct!

1. Who was Unai Emery manager of before he took over at Aston Villa?

 REAL BETIS    VILLARREAL

2. What was the main colour of West Ham's away kit in 2022-23?

 BLACK    ORANGE

3. Which Premier League team went on the longest unbeaten run in 2022-23?

NEWCASTLE    MAN. CITY

4. Which player scored more Premier League goals in 2022-23?

 HEUNG-MIN SON    RODRIGO

5. Who was one of the first two managers inducted into the PL Hall of Fame?

 JOSE MOURINHO   ARSENE WENGER

6. How many different teams have won the Premier League title?

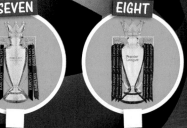 SEVEN   EIGHT

HIGHER OR LOWER?

Crystal Palace's Michael Olise bagged 11 PL assists in 2022-23! Did these stars get more or less?

1. James Maddison	HIGHER	LOWER
2. Mohamed Salah	HIGHER	LOWER
3. Leandro Trossard	HIGHER	LOWER
4. Pascal Gross	HIGHER	LOWER
5. Bryan Mbeumo	HIGHER	LOWER

BARMY BARNET

Which Prem star has got a wacky new haircut in this bonkers pic?

LEGENDARY

Which teams did these all-time legends play the most games for?

1. Eric Cantona

2. Mark Viduka

3. Tony Adams

4. Dion Dublin

5. Nicolas Anelka

6. Tim Cahill

CROSSWORD

Use the clues to fill in our Premier League crossword!

1. Colour of Aston Villa's third kit in 2022-23! (5)

3. Argentina CM who signed for Chelsea in January 2023 for over £100 million! (4,9)

5. Epic brand that produces the football for the Prem! (4)

7. Brighton's captain! (5,4)

8. Huge derby involving two teams from Liverpool! (10)

10. Name of Brentford's awesome bee mascot! (4)

11. Number of teams that get relegated from the Prem! (5)

12. Oldest current stadium in the Premier League! (7,4)

13. Legendary Newcastle player, _ _ _ _ _ Ginola! (5)

15. Former Premier League striker who played for both Liverpool and Chelsea! (8,6)

16. French club Wolves signed Mario Lemina from! (4)

17. Wales legend who starred for Tottenham in the PL! (6,4)

18. Number of Man. City players to score Prem hat-tricks in 2022-23! (3)

DOWN

1. Winners of the 1994-95 Premier League title! (9)

2. Number of Prem teams that Senegal legend Sadio Mane has played for! (3)

4. First-ever team to suffer PL relegation in 1992-93! (10,6)

6. The Premier League's top goalscorer in 2019-20! (5,5)

7. Position PL legend Ashley Cole used to play! (4,4)

9. Tottenham's nickname! (5)

14. African country Anass Zaroury plays for! (7)

ANSWERS ON PAGE 94

FOLLOW MATCH!

FOR LOADS OF AWESOME FOOTY NEWS, TRANSFER GOSSIP, VIDEOS & BANTER!

instagram.com/
matchmagofficial

tiktok.com/
matchmagofficial

twitter.com/
matchmagazine

facebook.com/
matchmagazine

You Tube

youtube.com/matchymovie

snapchat.com/add/
matchmagazine

CHECK OUT MATCH ON SOCIAL MEDIA RIGHT NOW!

ARGENTINA

FERNANDEZ

FACTFILE!

DOB: 17/01/01
Club: Chelsea
Country: Argentina
Position: Midfielder
Top Skill: Passing

Footy Fact! *World Cup-winning midfielder Enzo Fernandez is the second-youngest player ever (behind only Lionel Messi) to score a World Cup goal for Argentina!*

ULTIMATE GUIDE TO...
ENDRICK!

FAST FACTS

FOOTY IDOL
His football idol is none other than Real Madrid legend Cristiano Ronaldo! That will go down well with Los Blancos fans!

PALMEIRAS PRODIGY
He joined Palmeiras' youth team at the age of 11. In five years, he'd scored 165 goals in 169 games for the academy!

RECORD BREAKER
He made his professional debut in October 2022 at 16 years, two months and 16 days old, becoming the youngest player ever to appear for Palmeiras!

SCORING SENSATION
In the same month of his debut, he became the second-youngest goalscorer in the history of Brazil's first division!

MATCH tells you all you need to know about the youngster who's moving to REAL MADRID in 2024!

PLAYING STYLE!
Endrick is a left-footed forward who can play off the wing or as a central striker! As well as an eye for goal, he's got bundles of tricks up his sleeve, so he'll cause havoc alongside Brazil mates Vinicius Junior and Rodrygo. Another thing that won't go unnoticed is his work rate - he pesters defenders with his constant pressing!

WICKED WORLDIE
Endrick announced himself to the footy world when he was 15 years old at a 2022 youth tournament in Sao Paulo, Brazil! He scored seven goals in seven games and was voted Player of the Tournament after leading Palmeiras to the title, but it was one goal in particular that stood out - an overhead kick from outside of the box!

FACTFILE!
Full name: *Endrick Felipe Moreira de Sousa*
Club: *Palmeiras*
Age: 17
Position: *Forward*
Boot brand: *Nike*

Endrick isn't the only young Brazil baller on the rise!

MADRID MOVE!

In December 2022, Real Madrid confirmed an agreement with Palmeiras for a deal that could reach over £50 million with add-ons, although he can't join them officially until he turns 18 in July 2024! They had to beat tons of top European clubs for his signature, including Chelsea, who'd even hosted the youngster's family at their Cobham training centre!

IS HE THE NEXT... NEYMAR?

Endrick has already been compared to Brazilian greats like Ronaldo and Romario but we think he's got a touch of Neymar about him! Funnily enough, Neymar almost joined Real Madrid when he was a teenager before moving to Barcelona, so Los Blancos will be glad not to have let another future superstar get away!

ROBERT RENAN
Centre-Back

Renan signed for Russian Premier League club Zenit Saint Petersburg on a five-year contract in January 2023 but is already interesting Real Madrid scouts!

ARTHUR
Right-Back

The speedy right-back made his senior Brazil debut in March 2023, before joining German giants Bayer Leverkusen from America Mineiro over the summer!

ANDREY SANTOS
Midfielder

The Chelsea wonderkid captained Brazil's Under-20s en route to the 2023 South American U20 Championship title, finishing as joint-top scorer with six goals!

VITOR ROQUE
Striker

Quick, skilful, athletic and built like a brick wall, the hulking centre-forward bullies defenders and is rated really highly by Barcelona boss Xavi!

NOW TURN OVER FOR OUR PREMIER LEAGUE WONDERKID XI!

JOSKO GVARDIOL

Gvardiol has been known as one of the best young CBs in Europe ever since the summer of 2021 when he joined German outfit RB Leipzig from hometown club Dinamo Zagreb! He starred at the 2022 World Cup for Croatia and became the second-most expensive defender ever when he joined City last summer!

MICHAEL OLISE

At the age of just 21, Olise already has one of the sweetest left feet in the Premier League! Whether he's slicing open a defence with a quality pass or lashing in a long-range shot, he's absolutely deadly! Palace fans are buzzing after he signed a new four-year contract with the club last summer!

BEN DOAK

The Scottish teenager is one of the worst-kept secrets on Merseyside - everyone in Liverpool knows he's gonna be a star! The Reds spent £600,000 to land him from Celtic in March 2022, and he became the PL's youngest-ever Scottish player the following December. Despite his tender years, he already has the strength, pace and tekkers to tear full-backs apart!

James Trafford
Burnley & England

Rico Lewis
Man. City & England

Josko Gvardiol
Man. City & Croatia

Michael Olise
Crystal Palace & France

Moises Caicedo
Chelsea & Ecuador

Ben Doak
Liverpool & Scotland

Evan Ferguson
Brighton & Republic of Ireland

ERKID XI

ALEX SCOTT

When he first broke through at Bristol City, Scott was compared with Jack Grealish because of his silky dribbling, creativity and ability to win free-kicks. But since then he's developed into a proper all-round midfielder, and has even played at right wing-back for the Robins! Bournemouth paid £25m to land the wonderkid, who starred in England U19s' victory at the European Championship in 2022!

Levi Colwill
Chelsea & England

Destiny Udogie
Tottenham & Italy

Alex Scott
Bournemouth & England

ALEJANDRO GARNACHO

2024 could be a massive year for Garnacho. In the 19 Prem games that he played for United last season, he proved that he's a top-class dribbler with the tricks, flicks and flair to give any defender nightmares! There's just one problem for The Red Devils – he plays in the same position as top goalscorer Marcus Rashford!

Alejandro Garnacho
Man. United & Argentina

THE SUBS' BENCH

 **GK**

Bart Verbruggen
Brighton & Netherlands

 **FB**

Ian Maatsen
Chelsea & Netherlands

 **CB**

Jarrad Branthwaite
Everton & England

 **DM**

Romeo Lavia
Chelsea & Belgium

 **CM**

Stefan Bajcetic
Liverpool & Spain

 **FW**

Julio Enciso
Brighton & Paraguay

 **FW**

Rasmus Hojlund
Man. United & Denmark

BUKAYO SAKA

THE GUNNERS' STAR BOY!

FACTPACK

DOB: *05/09/01*
Club: *Arsenal*
Country: *England*
Position: *Winger*
Boots: *New Balance Furon*
Top Skill: *Flawless technique*

SKILLS

Saka's left foot is one of the best in the world, capable of playing a pass, picking a cross or drilling a shot! His brilliant footy brain means he always makes the right decision and gets into brilliant positions! He doesn't use loads of tricks to get past defenders, but beats them with his directness, pace, acceleration and agility!

STORY

Saka has been at Arsenal since he was seven years old, and made his first-team debut ten years later. As soon as he stepped onto the pitch he looked like a future star, and it didn't take long for him to become a key player for both club and country! The 2022-23 season was his best so far – he bagged 14 goals and 11 assists as Arsenal almost won the Prem title!

Take a look at some of Saka's best moments...

Arsenal v Qarabag, 2018

Even at the tender age of 17, the youngster looked ready to be an Arsenal superstar from his very first start for The Gunners!

STYLE

Some wingers like getting the ball to feet and dribbling to commit defenders, while others make runs to stretch defences and get on the end of chances – but Saka is special because he loves to do both! With flawless technique, electric pace and a genius footy brain, the Arsenal ace is the complete package, and is always capable of making things happen. Plus, to top it all, he plays with a massive smile on his face!

Arsenal v Tottenham, 2021

First he set up his old mate Emile Smith Rowe, then notched one for himself against Arsenal's biggest rivals!

HE PLAYS LIKE...
Sadio Mane

The Arsenal superstar is like a left-footed version of Mane! The Senegal legend terrorised Prem defences for years with his pace and skill, and Saka looks like he's ready to do the same!

England v France, 2022

After scoring three WC goals – versus Iran and Senegal – Saka was England's Man of the Match in their gutting quarter-final loss!

Arsenal v Man. United, 2023

The winger showed his magic here by scoring a long-range worldie out of absolutely nothing!

WHAT'S IN STORE FOR 2024?

Saka will be one of the first names on the teamsheet for both Arsenal and England as they go hunting for silverware in 2024! He's been brilliant for club and country over the last few seasons and, at the age of 22, he's only going to get better and better! All The Gunners' star boy needs now is some trophies to top it off!

England v North Macedonia, 2023

All three of Saka's goals in the first-ever hat-trick of his career were absolutely elite finishes, especially his thunderous second!

BIG MATCH QUIZ!

How many of these Euro league brain-busters can you get right?

6 QUESTIONS ON...

1 Before 2022-23, when was the last time they won the Serie A title – 1970, 1980, 1990 or 2000?

2 True or False? Their stadium is named after footy legend Diego Maradona!

3 What country does wing wizard Khvicha Kvaratskhelia play for?

4 Which of these is one of their nicknames – The Little Bears, The Little Donkeys, The Little Eagles or The Little Elephants?

5 Name their lethal top goalscorer from the 2022-23 campaign!

6 True or False? They released a special-edition shirt for Valentine's Day in 2023!

1.

2.

CLSE-UP!

Can you name these four Clasico superstars we've zoomed in on?

3.

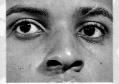

4.

CRAZY KIT!

Which European giants once wore this eye-boggling pink strip?

ODD ONE OUT!

SCHALKE

STOKE

MAINZ

LYON

Which of these clubs has forward Eric Maxim Choupo-Moting never turned out for during his awesome career?

ACE ACTIVITY

FOOTY MISMATCH

Spot ten differences between these two Ligue 1 pics!

ANSWERS ON PAGE 94

INTERNATIONAL

Think about which colours each country normally wears!

GET DRAWING RIGHT NOW!

MATCH wants you to design three international shirts for the 2024 European Championship! Rather than creating the home, away and third shirt for one country, we want you to design one shirt for three different nations! So pick your three countries and get creative!

SEND IT IN!

Make sure you send your designs to MATCH - by email match.magazine@kelsey.co.uk or via social media - and we'll feature our faves in the mag!

COUNTRY 1:

SHIRT DESIGNS!

Go as simple or as wacky as you want – we don't mind!

Don't forget to put the country's crest on the shirt!

COUNTRY 2:

COUNTRY 3:

EURO 2024 DREAM TEAM!

Imagine you could take a team to Germany for *EURO 2024* using a mix of players from all over Europe! Take a look through the superstars we've picked out, then select your favourite line-up on page 46...

EURO 2024 DREAM TEAM
GOALKEEPERS!

GIANLUIGI DONNARUMMA
ITALY

At Euro 2020, Donnarumma became the first goalkeeper to be named the official Player of the Tournament, so if anyone knows about delivering at this level it's him! He kept three clean sheets in seven games, but more importantly saved two crucial spot-kicks in the final penalty shootout against England as Italy got their hands on the trophy!

JORDAN PICKFORD
ENGLAND

England have produced some of their best-ever performances at the last three major tournaments, and nobody's played more minutes in that time than Pickford! He's a brilliant shot stopper with top reflexes, but what really sets him apart is his kicking - his left foot can ping the ball anywhere on the pitch!

THIBAUT COURTOIS
BELGIUM

You only have to look at Courtois' stack of medals to see why people reckon he's the best keeper in the world! He's won a Champions League, league titles with Atletico, Chelsea and Real Madrid, plus loads of individual awards. He's so big and dominant, attackers just don't believe they'll score against him!

UNAI SIMON
SPAIN

The Athletic Bilbao keeper has been so classy for his country over the last few years that he's pushed David De Gea completely out of the Spain squad. Unlike De Gea, Simon loves playing out from the back so he's perfect for La Roja's passing style, but he's also capable of pulling off unreal saves too!

MIKE MAIGNAN
FRANCE

France had a big hole to fill when their legendary GK Hugo Lloris retired from international duty in 2022, but Maignan has been the perfect replacement! He was a hero in Lille's shock Ligue 1 title win in 2020-21, did the same thing for Milan after joining them and has taken that form to the national team too!

BEST OF THE REST!
CHECK OUT THESE OTHER SUPERSTARS!

MARC-ANDRE TER STEGEN
Germany

JAN OBLAK
Slovenia

WOJCIECH SZCZESNY
Poland

MANUEL NEUER
Germany

Now pick your Euro 2024 Dream Team goalkeeper!

TURN TO PAGE 46

EURO 2024 DREAM TEAM
CENTRE-BACKS!

DAVID ALABA
AUSTRIA

The Austria captain has played all over the pitch - from the left wing to central midfield to left-back - but these days he's happiest at CB. He's a super smart player, reads the game brilliantly and has loads of quality in his left foot, plus his versatility means you can pick him almost anywhere in your team!

LEONARDO BONUCCI
ITALY

Italy's captain probably knows more about defending than any other player in Europe! He could be in his country's top three most-capped players by the time the Euros kick off, but don't just consider him for his experience - his passing range is world class too!

DANILO PEREIRA
PORTUGAL

For most of his career Danilo was a rock-solid DM, but since joining PSG in 2020 he's dropped back into defence. He's always been a beast that loves crunching into tackles, but playing deeper allows him to ping passes around too - so if you want your team to play out from the back, get him in!

JOSKO GVARDIOL
CROATIA

The 21-year-old is one of the best young defenders in Europe - as he proved by being one of the World Cup's standout players as Croatia marched to the semi-finals at Qatar 2022. He's a world-class centre-back, but is also comfortable playing at left-back!

WILLIAM SALIBA
FRANCE

France have so many options at centre-back, we could have filled most of this page with their players! Saliba doesn't have too many caps just yet, and only made his international debut in 2022, but if he stays fit and in-form for Arsenal then he'll be banging on the door big-time by the Euros!

BEST OF THE REST!
CHECK OUT THESE OTHER SUPERSTARS!

JOHN STONES
England

MILAN SKRINIAR
Slovakia

RUBEN DIAS
Portugal

VIRGIL VAN DIJK
Netherlands

ANTONIO RUDIGER
Germany

KYLE WALKER

ENGLAND

With Kieran Trippier, Reece James and Trent Alexander-Arnold, England have tons of attacking options at right-back, but Walker is usually their first choice because of his world-class defensive quality and recovery pace! He's one of the quickest players on the planet, so even the best wingers can't beat him!

OLEKSANDR ZINCHENKO

UKRAINE

If Ukraine make it to the Euros then we'll probably see Zinchenko lining up in central midfield, but for Arsenal he's brilliant at left-back. Mikel Arteta asks him to drift into the middle of the pitch, and from there he can boss games with his intelligence and range of passing!

GIOVANNI DI LORENZO

ITALY

For the last few years, Di Lorenzo has been one of the most consistent defenders in Italy! He was first-choice right-back when his country won Euro 2020, and in 2022-23 he captained Napoli to their first Serie A title win in 33 years! He's a solid tackler and has plenty of quality going forward!

ALEJANDRO BALDE

SPAIN

Jordi Alba has been a world-class left-back for years – and he's still going strong – but now Barcelona and Spain have found his long-term replacement. Like Alba, Balde loves to get forward on the overlap and create chances for attackers, while the youngster's pace makes him tough to dribble past too!

THEO HERNANDEZ

FRANCE

There aren't many more exciting full-backs on the planet than Theo. He's ridiculously quick, and uses that electric pace to fly up the left wing and terrify opposition defences. He's scored some absolute worldies for his club AC Milan – go and check them out on YouTube!

LUKE SHAW
England

JOAO CANCELO
Portugal

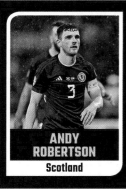

ANDY ROBERTSON
Scotland

JULES KOUNDE
France

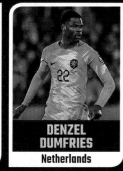

DENZEL DUMFRIES
Netherlands

Now pick your Euro 2024 Dream Team centre-backs & full-backs!

TURN TO PAGE 46

MATCH! 41

EURO 2024 DREAM TEAM
CENTRAL MIDFIELDERS!

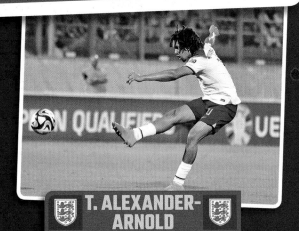

LUKA MODRIC
CROATIA

If Croatia make it to the Euros then make the most of watching Modric, because it could be his last tournament. Then again, the 38-year-old hasn't looked like slowing down over the last few years and continues to dominate midfields with his footy genius, quick feet and brilliant passing ability!

RODRI
SPAIN

The Man. City man is probably the best holding midfielder in the world! That's because he's brilliant at snuffing out opposition attacks, hardly ever gives the ball away and can even pop up with the odd goal – as he showed in the 2023 Champions League final!

T. ALEXANDER-ARNOLD
ENGLAND

You could pick Trent at right-back, but England boss Gareth Southgate tried him in midfield in 2023 and he totally bossed it! Whatever position he plays, he's one of the most creative players on the planet, is a set-piece demon and can bag assists from anywhere!

JOSHUA KIMMICH
GERMANY

Like Trent, Kimmich has played plenty of football at right-back, but now likes to run games from the middle of the park for club and country! He racks up tons of assists thanks to his passing range, crossing ability and set-piece taking, plus his experience in defence means he loves a monster tackle, too!

DOMINIK SZOBOSZLAI
HUNGARY

Hungary supporters were gutted when Szoboszlai missed Euro 2020 through injury. Although he was only 20 at the time, he was already their main man and since then has only got better! The Liverpool ace loves shooting from long range and is a deadly free-kick taker!

BEST OF THE REST!
CHECK OUT THESE OTHER SUPERSTARS!

GRANIT XHAKA
Switzerland

ILKAY GUNDOGAN
Germany

DECLAN RICE
England

MARTIN ODEGAARD
Norway

MARCO VERRATTI
Italy

KEVIN DE BRUYNE
BELGIUM

You don't need us to tell you how good KDB is – he's been bossing the Prem for years and is one of Belgium's all-time greats! The Man. City legend scores and creates goals out of absolutely nothing with either foot, so he terrifies opponents whenever he gets on the ball!

JAMAL MUSIALA
GERMANY

One of Musiala's biggest strengths is his versatility, so you could easily pick him as a CAM or left-winger. We love watching him in central midfield though, because every time he gets on the ball he looks to drive forward through the middle of the pitch, take players on and make things happen for his team!

PEDRI
SPAIN

With the help of his Barca and Spain team-mate Gavi, Pedri is capable of keeping the ball all day long! Sometimes he plays out wide, but he's much better in the middle of the pitch where he can get on the ball, make things happen and create chances for his team!

XAVI SIMONS
NETHERLANDS

If you want to include some wicked wonderkids in your team, then you have to take a look at Simons! The 20-year-old attacking midfielder was unstoppable in his sole season at PSV, bagging 19 goals and eight assists in the league, and looks set to be a huge star for his country too!

EDUARDO CAMAVINGA
FRANCE

Camavinga has played plenty of games at left-back for both France and Real Madrid, but his future is in midfield. With pace, energy, a great left foot and top-class tackling and dribbling ability, he's almost the perfect player – he just needs to score more goals!

BERNARDO SILVA
Portugal

FRENKIE DE JONG
Netherlands

SCOTT McTOMINAY
Scotland

BRUNO FERNANDES
Portugal

JUDE BELLINGHAM
England

Now pick your Euro 2024 Dream Team midfielders!

TURN TO PAGE 46

EURO 2024 DREAM TEAM
FORWARDS!

KYLIAN MBAPPE

FRANCE

How do you stop a player like Mbappe? He's one of the quickest players we've ever seen but, even if defenders do manage to keep up with him, he's got the skills and agility to tie them in knots! Then when he gets a sight of goal, he's deadly – surely everyone will pick the France legend in their team!

CRISTIANO RONALDO

PORTUGAL

He might be in his late 30s and no longer playing his club footy in Europe, but CR7 will still have a big part to play at Euro 2024! He's already played more games, scored more goals and won more matches than any player in the comp's history, and will be chasing even more records in Germany next summer!

CODY GAKPO

NETHERLANDS

The young Dutchman burst onto the scene as an electric winger that could fly down the flanks and create goals, but since he's joined Liverpool Jurgen Klopp has converted him into a false nine or centre-forward that can drop deep, link attacks and get on the end of chances!

MARCUS RASHFORD

ENGLAND

The 2022-23 season was the best of Rashford's career, as he notched 30 goals in all comps for the first time, as well as bagging three at the World Cup. If he keeps that form up in 2024, he'll be well on his way to becoming a Man. United and England legend!

ANSU FATI

SPAIN

After loads of injury problems, Fati played over 30 La Liga games in the 2022-23 season for the first time in his career! The winger became Barcelona's youngest-ever La Liga goalscorer at the age of 16, and is still one of the most exciting wonderkids in the world – hopefully he'll show why at the Euros!

BEST OF THE REST!
CHECK OUT THESE OTHER SUPERSTARS!

RAFAEL LEAO
Portugal

ALEXANDER ISAK
Sweden

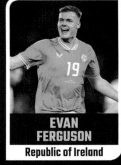
EVAN FERGUSON
Republic of Ireland

ROMELU LUKAKU
Belgium

BUKAYO SAKA
England

HARRY KANE

ENGLAND

No European player has scored more goals at the last three major tournaments than Kane with 12, so if you want someone to deliver at the Euros then he's your man! England's record goalscorer is also a top captain and a quality creator of chances too!

PATRIK SCHICK

CZECH REPUBLIC

Nobody scored more goals than Schick at Euro 2020, while his halfway-line stunner against Scotland was named Goal of the Tournament! He followed that up by banging in 24 goals in just 27 Bundesliga games, before injuries totally ruined his 2022-23 campaign!

ERLING HAALAND

NORWAY

We're desperate for Norway to qualify for their first major tournament since 1998 just to see if Haaland can boss international defences like he does in the Premier League! His bonkers tally of 36 Prem goals in 2022-23 was a new record and, at the age of 23, he's only going to get better. Scary!

FEDERICO CHIESA

ITALY

Chiesa was one of the stars of Euro 2020, scoring two goals for the champions and bagging a spot in the Team of the Tournament, but since then he's had terrible injuries. He returned to the Juventus line-up at the end of 2022-23 and scored for Italy in the 2023 Nations League finals, so he could have a big 2024 ahead of him!

ANTOINE GRIEZMANN

FRANCE

Grizi starred in midfield on France's run to the 2022 WC final, but he was back up front when he returned to Atletico Madrid and notched loads of goals and assists! He'll be 33 when the Euros kick off, but he's still got enough quality in that left boot to fire France to glory!

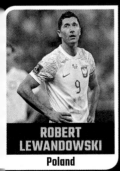

ROBERT LEWANDOWSKI
Poland

RASMUS HOJLUND
Denmark

KHVICHA KVARATSKHELIA
Georgia

GONCALO RAMOS
Portugal

ALEKSANDAR MITROVIC
Serbia

Now pick your Euro 2024 Dream Team forwards!

TURN OVER NOW...

MY EURO 2024 DREAM TEAM!

Now you've seen some of Europe's top stars, write your selections below then put them in whatever formation you want! You don't just have to pick players from our shortlist!

MY PLAYERS!

ENGLAND

KELLY

ATTACK-TICS

MATCH breaks down the attacking tactics of the Premier League's greatest title winners!

Premier League

BLACKBURN
1994-95

Manager
Kenny Dalglish

Flowers

Berg — Pearce — Hendry — Le Saux

Ripley — Sherwood — Atkins — Wilcox

Shearer — Sutton

ROAD TO THE TITLE!

Blackburn Rovers spent big in the early '90s under owner Jack Walker to build the best squad in the country, and they were rewarded with the Premier League title in 1995! They had quality throughout the team, but the stars were strike partners Alan Shearer and Chris Sutton, who scored 49 goals between them with Shearer netting 34 alone – a PL record until last season!

HOW THEY WORKED!

⚽ Sutton and Shearer – aka SAS – were both tall, strong and powerful strikers that absolutely dominated opposition centre-backs!

⚽ They fed on quality crosses from electric wingers Stuart Ripley and Jason Wilcox and England international left-back Graeme Le Saux!

⚽ SAS weren't just goalscorers, they had great link-up play too – that's why they both bagged double figures for assists!

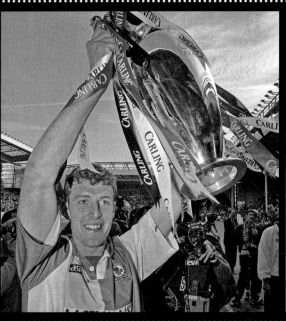

MAN. UNITED
1998-99

Manager
Alex Ferguson

Schmeichel

G. Neville — Johnsen — Stam — Irwin

Beckham — Scholes — Keane — Giggs

Cole — Yorke

ROAD TO THE TITLE!

Not only did United win the Premier League, they also won the FA Cup and Champions League – making them the first English team to win the treble! They did it thanks to having a top squad – including the likes of Nicky Butt, Phil Neville, Teddy Sheringham, Jesper Blomqvist, Ole Gunnar Solskjaer and Henning Berg – which Ferguson regularly rotated to keep his players fresh!

HOW THEY WORKED!

⚽ United played a classic 4-4-2, where all the midfielders were proper box-to-box players that ran up and down all game!

⚽ Crossing was a big part of their gameplan, especially from the right where David Beckham produced world-class deliveries!

⚽ United had four top strikers, but Dwight Yorke and Andy Cole's partnership ruled – defences couldn't cope with their movement!

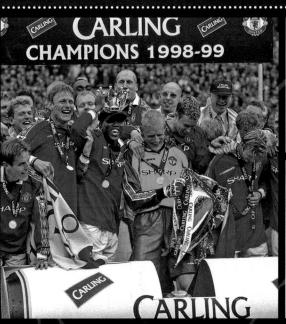

ARSENAL
2003-04

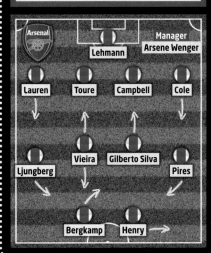

Manager
Arsene Wenger

Lehmann

Lauren — Toure — Campbell — Cole

Ljungberg — Vieira — Gilberto Silva — Pires

Bergkamp — Henry

ROAD TO THE TITLE!

This is another campaign that's gone down in the history books, as Arsenal went through the entire season without losing a single game – the only team in Premier League history to do so! The 'Invincibles', as they're known, did it in style too, playing fast attacking football with Gunners legend Thierry Henry leading the way with 30 goals and six assists!

HOW THEY WORKED!

⚽ Both The Gunners' full-backs loved to fly forward and join in with the attacks!

⚽ With the two DMs totally bossing midfield, Dennis Bergkamp dropped deep as a CAM and Henry drifted out to the left wing. Fluid!

⚽ Henry loved linking up with Pires, who would often cut inside to grab goals, while Ashley Cole provided the width with Henry – opposition right-backs got torn apart by The Gunners!

MAN. UNITED
2007-08

Manager
Alex Ferguson

Van der Sar

Brown — Ferdinand — Vidic — Evra

Scholes — Carrick

Ronaldo — Tevez — Giggs

Rooney

ROAD TO THE TITLE!

This was the season that made the world realise just how special Cristiano Ronaldo was going to be! He won his first Ballon d'Or after powering United to the title with 31 goals in just 34 games – but he had plenty of help from some brilliant team-mates, including one of the best attacking trios in Prem history and one of the most solid defences which provided the foundation!

HOW THEY WORKED!

⚽ With a rock-hard back four and two world-class passers in central midfield, The Red Devils' forwards had total freedom!

⚽ Ronaldo started on the wing but swapped positions with Wayne Rooney or Carlos Tevez to confuse opponents and create space!

⚽ United were the first English team to play with a 'false nine' – Rooney and Tevez roamed everywhere to create space for CR7!

CHELSEA
2009-10

Manager
Carlo Ancelotti

Cech

Ivanovic — Carvalho — Terry — Cole

Makelele

Ballack — Lampard

Anelka — Malouda

Drogba

ROAD TO THE TITLE!

Legendary manager Carlo Ancelotti won the Premier League in his first season in England, ending Man. United's run of three consecutive crowns! It was close – they won the title by just one point – but they did it with a record-breaking tally of 103 goals thanks to an 8-0 win on the final day! It was a record that stood until Man. City broke it in 2017-18!

HOW THEY WORKED!

⚽ Chelsea used different formations in this season, most frequently switching between a 4-3-3 and a 4-4-2 diamond!

⚽ Club legend Frank Lampard set up six of Didier Drogba's 29 Premier League goals – their partnership was key!

⚽ Nicolas Anelka chipped in with vital goals as well – especially when Drogba was away on AFCON duty with the Ivory Coast!

LEICESTER
2015-16

Manager
Claudio Ranieri

Schmeichel

Simpson — Morgan — Huth — Fuchs

Mahrez — Kante — Drinkwater — Albrighton

Vardy — Okazaki

ROAD TO THE TITLE!

In the greatest underdog story the Premier League has ever seen, Leicester went from narrowly avoiding relegation in 2014-15 to lifting the title a year later! The Foxes were a well-organised and hard-working team regularly starting the same XI, with individual stars like Kasper Schmeichel, N'Golo Kante, Riyad Mahrez and Jamie Vardy making the difference!

HOW THEY WORKED!

⚽ Leicester weren't bothered at all about keeping the ball – only two Premier League sides had less possession during that season!

⚽ They sat deep until lung-busting tackling machine Kante won the ball back, then quickly sprung forward and attacked!

⚽ When speed machine Vardy didn't have space to run into, Mahrez could always provide some magic from the wing!

MAN. CITY
2017-18

Manager Pep Guardiola

Ederson

Walker — Otamendi — Kompany — Delph

Fernandinho

De Bruyne — D. Silva

Sterling — Aguero — Sane

ROAD TO THE TITLE!

In his first Premier League title win, Pep Guardiola's team smashed loads of records that are still standing to this day! They were the first team to reach 100 points and scored a whopping 106 goals, while the league's top four assisters were all City players – creative talents Kevin De Bruyne, Leroy Sane, David Silva and Raheem Sterling!

HOW THEY WORKED!

⚽ City controlled games because they hardly ever gave the ball away, averaging 66% possession during the 2017-18 campaign!

⚽ With all the ball, City could use two playmakers in central midfield, and De Bruyne and Silva created loads of chances!

⚽ The pacy wingers stayed high and wide, then darted into the penalty box when the team attacked to get on the end of crosses!

LIVERPOOL
2019-20

Manager Jurgen Klopp

Alisson

Alexander-Arnold — Gomez — Van Dijk — Robertson

Fabinho

Henderson — Wijnaldum

Salah — Firmino — Mane

ROAD TO THE TITLE!

Liverpool's famous win in 2019-20 put an end to a very long wait for Reds supporters – they hadn't seen their team win the league title for 30 years, and never during the Premier League era! But mastermind Jurgen Klopp changed all that, delivering the crown thanks to the high-pressing tactics he'd developed in Germany known as 'gegenpressing'. Legend!

HOW THEY WORKED!

⚽ Liverpool's front three were brilliant at pressing their opponents, and attacked as soon as they won the ball back in the final third!

⚽ Number nine Roberto Firmino dropped deep, while Mohamed Salah and Sadio Mane attacked from the wings to devastating effect!

⚽ Full-backs Trent Alexander-Arnold and Andy Robertson flew forward to grab assists while the midfield covered for them!

MAN. CITY
2022-23

Manager Pep Guardiola

Ederson

Akanji — Dias — Ake

Stones — Rodri

B. Silva — De Bruyne — Gundogan — Grealish

Haaland

ROAD TO THE TITLE!

With Arsenal leading the league for most of the season – 248 days, which is a record for a team that failed to go on and capture the title – Pep Guardiola had to come up with something special. Not only did the Spanish coach's genius tactical plan help City catch The Gunners, it also won them the Champions League and FA Cup too as they went on to do the treble!

HOW THEY WORKED!

⚽ Instead of using attacking, overlapping full-backs, City started playing four centre-backs – players that would each win their duels!

⚽ Centre-back John Stones stepped up into midfield next to Rodri to make the team more solid and boss possession!

⚽ That left the other creative midfielders free to lay chances on a plate for the absolute goal machine up top, Erling Haaland!

BIG MATCH QUIZ!

How many of these mind-boggling EFL teasers can you get right?

FOOTY MAZE

Which route reunites Bolton with their EFL Trophy?

A   B   C

PLAYER BATTLE!

Who scored more Championship goals during the 2022-23 campaign?

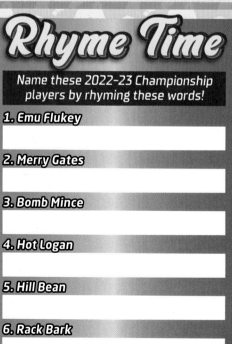

Viktor Gyokeres	✔	
v		
Chuba Akpom	✔	
Joel Piroe	✔	
v		
Tom Bradshaw	✔	
Carlton Morris	✔	
v		
Iliman Ndiaye	✔	
Ben Brereton Diaz	✔	
v		
Nathan Tella	✔	
Oscar Estupinan	✔	
v		
Tyrece Campbell	✔	

Rhyme Time

Name these 2022-23 Championship players by rhyming these words!

1. Emu Flukey

2. Merry Gates

3. Bomb Mince

4. Hot Logan

5. Hill Bean

6. Rack Bark

KIT CLASH!

Which Watford superstar has been cloned wearing a West Brom shirt?

WORDFIT

Can you fit these English Football League teams into the mega grid below?

Barnsley	Charlton	Crewe	Huddersfield	Rotherham
Blackpool	Colchester	Derby	Ipswich	Walsall
Bolton	Coventry	Forest Green	Lincoln	Wigan
Cardiff	Crawley	Harrogate	Portsmouth	Wycombe

ANSWERS ON PAGE 94

SNAPPED!
BEST OF 2023!

Celebration copycats!

LET'S GO, BRO!

Brennan Johnson and Morgan Gibbs-White are two peas in a pod!

Hitching a ride!

We hope Nathan Ake is going to tip for that private taxi service!

WHERE TO, MATE?

Jokin' Jesse!

SHOULDN'T THESE BE SMALLER?

We're not sure those are the best cones for the warm-up drills, Jesse…

Round one!

PUT 'EM UP, MATCH!

In the claret corner, it's Ollie Watkins…

Leaning tower of Leeds!

HANG IN THERE, TYLER!

Tyler Adams needs a replacement back after that aerial duel!

Toilet emergency!

DON'T MAKE ME LAUGH, MAN!

Gnonto regrets drinking that extra bottle of Lucozade!

Dribble king!

Joe Willock's dribbling style is definitely unique!

TRY GETTING IT OFF ME NOW!

Silly Seagulls!

WE'RE OFF TO STEAL SOME CHIPS!

These Brighton supporters lived up to their nickname!

WWE!

Frenkie de Jong needs to work on his body slam!

HE'S GOT ME IN A HEADLOCK!

Groovy Gunner!

HELP, PLEASE!

Arsenal's Steph Catley got herself into a right tangle!

Hair obstruction!

Alisha Lehmann needed 5kg of gel to make it stay like that!

AND IT'S THE MEGA HOLD!

Bear-ware!

SHHH, THEY'RE MY LUNCH!

Did the Rennes' players know there was a big bear behind them?

KHVICHA KVARATSKHELIA

THE NUTMEG MASTER!

FACTPACK

DOB: *12/02/01*
Club: *Napoli*
Country: *Georgia*
Position: *Winger*
Boots: *Nike Mercurial*
Top Skill: *Silky dribbling*

STYLE

Wearing his classy Napoli kit with his socks rolled down, Khvicha has serious drip! But he's not a flashy player that shows off his tricks for nothing – when he's running with the ball, all he thinks about is making something happen for his team! The Georgia superstar always plays with his head up, so he can spot a team-mate in space for a pass or a gap in the defence that he can dribble through!

SKILLS

When it comes to one-on-one dribbling, there aren't many players on the planet that are better than Kvaratskhelia! His classy touch and brilliant balance gives him total control over his markers, plus he's a master of nutmegs! When he gets into dangerous positions, he delivers – he was directly involved in 22 Serie A goals in 2022-23, bagging some real worldies!

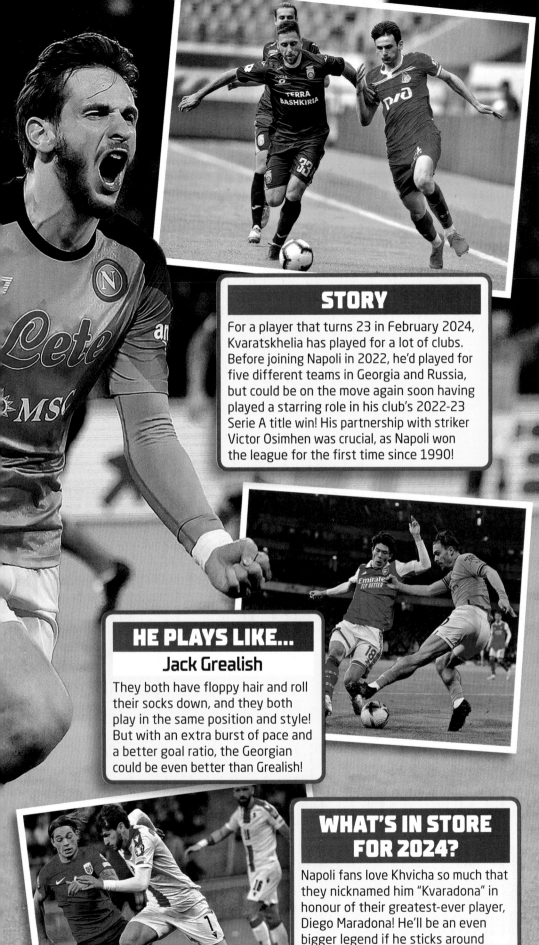

STORY

For a player that turns 23 in February 2024, Kvaratskhelia has played for a lot of clubs. Before joining Napoli in 2022, he'd played for five different teams in Georgia and Russia, but could be on the move again soon having played a starring role in his club's 2022-23 Serie A title win! His partnership with striker Victor Osimhen was crucial, as Napoli won the league for the first time since 1990!

HE PLAYS LIKE...
Jack Grealish

They both have floppy hair and roll their socks down, and they both play in the same position and style! But with an extra burst of pace and a better goal ratio, the Georgian could be even better than Grealish!

WHAT'S IN STORE FOR 2024?

Napoli fans love Khvicha so much that they nicknamed him "Kvaradona" in honour of their greatest-ever player, Diego Maradona! He'll be an even bigger legend if he sticks around at the Italian club in 2024, while his national team Georgia are dreaming of reaching their first-ever major tournament at the Euros in Germany!

SHOW REEL!

Take a look at some of Kvaratskhelia's best moments...

Georgia v Spain, 2021

Spanish defenders looked terrified every time Khvicha got on the ball, and he topped off his performance with a brilliant goal!

Napoli v Liverpool, 2022

Kvaratskhelia gave Trent Alexander-Arnold a torrid time in Napoli's 4-1 home win over Liverpool in the 2022-23 Champo League!

Napoli v Ajax, 2022

Ajax's defence got totally shredded by Kvaratskhelia too, as he showed he can beat players with pace as well as trickery!

Sassuolo v Napoli, 2023

After picking up the ball on the halfway line, he skipped past two challenges and drilled a shot into the bottom corner!

Napoli v Atalanta, 2023

With one movement, Kvaradona's dummy sent three defenders for a pie before he smashed the ball into the top corner!

PEDRI
SPAIN

KYLIAN MBAPPE
FRANCE

RETRO BALLERS!

MATCH imagines what these Euro superstars would look like if they went back in time. LOL!

ROBERT LEWANDOWSKI
POLAND

GIANLUIGI DONNARUMMA
ITALY

DECLAN RICE
ENGLAND

DAVID ALABA
AUSTRIA

JAMAL MUSIALA
GERMANY

SCOTT McTOMINAY
SCOTLAND

MANUEL AKANJI
SWITZERLAND

JOAO FELIX
PORTUGAL

MATCH! CHATS TO THE STARS!

MATCH chatted to tons of footy superstars in 2022-23! Get a load of the best quotes that featured in our magazine over the past 12 months...

SVEN BOTMAN

The Newcastle centre-back was a huge FIFA fan when he was a child...

BOTMAN SAYS: "When I was younger, I used to get the new FIFA game and I would spend hours playing it - even when all my family were there! They were understanding as they knew I was just crazy about football. It is cool to think that some kids get FIFA and play as Newcastle with me in their team - hopefully I can help them win!"

OLIVER SKIPP

The Tottenham academy gem told MATCH about an old Christmas tradition in the Skipp household...

SKIPP SAYS: "When I was younger, we had a treasure hunt for one of our presents. My sister and I would get quite competitive! My dad would send us to random places throughout the house and it would all lead back to one present. We'd both end up with something, but it was a race to see who'd get there first. It was cool!"

MARY FOWLER

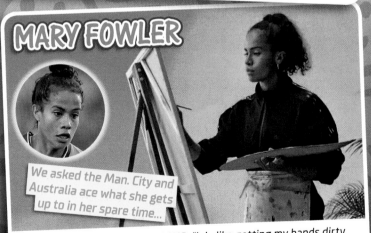

We asked the Man. City and Australia ace what she gets up to in her spare time...

FOWLER SAYS: "I do like getting my hands dirty when it comes to art! Right now I'm into clay moulding. I had some of the Man. City girls over at my place and we made some clay designs. I made a hand that holds jewellery. I like creating stuff, painting and drawing - it's what I do off the field if I have the time!"

ROBERT LEWANDOWSKI

The Barcelona star revealed that he wants to stay in football once he retires...

LEWANDOWSKI SAYS: "I have a lot of things to do in life, not just football! But for me, I want to stay in football when I retire because, with all my experience, I want to be able to help and give advice. I don't know what that role might be, but at least part of my life will have something to do with football!"

JACK GREALISH

The Man. City and England hero revealed some secrets after being revealed as a new Puma ambassador...

GREALISH SAYS: "My second favourite sport behind football is definitely tennis. I'm not that mad into other sports, but I do love the tennis. It's something that I want to get good at and start having lessons. Not be top, top – but something that I'd like to do as a little hobby. I would love to go to Wimbledon one day!"

KELLY SMITH

The Lionesses legend told MATCH about how the women's game has grown since she retired...

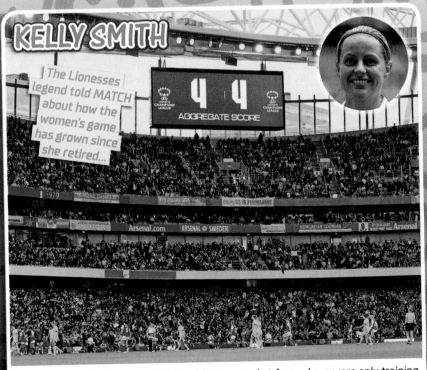

SMITH SAYS: "When I first started at Arsenal, we were only training two evenings a week and could only use the facility when the youth team had gone, so you didn't feel fully respected. Now they're at the men's training ground, training full-time and with physio access. The stadiums we played at were non-league, with a couple of hundred people, as people just didn't know about the women's game!"

ALEX IWOBI

The Everton ace gave MATCH some insight into what food he eats at Christmas...

IWOBI SAYS: "There will be a roast dinner with turkey, but my mum will also make so many different Nigerian dishes. There are yams, jollof rice, plantain...she really spoils us, which is why I always look forward to it! There are a good six dishes, a feast!"

DJED SPENCE

We asked the England Under-21 right-back what superpower he'd most like to possess...

SPENCE SAYS: "To stop time! I could do many things with that power. If I'm late to work, I'd stop time and drive through all the traffic. It could be useful on the pitch as well - if the opponents are going to score, you could stop time and remove the ball!"

TINO LIVRAMENTO

We asked the England Under-21 ace what his favourite-ever Christmas present was...

LIVRAMENTO SAYS: "I can't highlight one present, but getting any new football shirt growing up was always really special. I think I asked for a shirt pretty much every year when I was younger, and I never got bored of getting one each Christmas!"

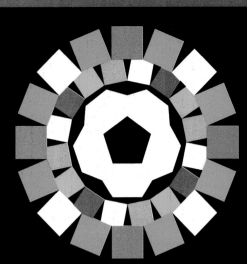

WOMEN'S WORLD CUP 2023 *Scrapbook!*

Last summer's *Women's World Cup* was awesome! Check out some of the biggest moments...

HEROIC HOSTS!

Co-hosts New Zealand were huge underdogs against Norway in the tournament's opener, but they showed incredible courage and commitment to win the game 1-0 through a really well worked team goal!

SIZZLING SAMBA STAR'S TREBLE!

Ary Borges became the youngest player in Women's World Cup history to score a hat-trick on her tourno debut at 23 years old, as Brazil earned a 4-0 victory over debutants Panama. She also produced an ace roll-back assist in what was an epic team goal!

HISTORY MAKER!

South Korea's Casey Phair became the youngest-ever player at a Women's World Cup in their loss to Colombia! The forward, aged 16 years and 26 days, was introduced as a 77th-minute substitute!

E.T. PHONE HOME!

Germany captain Alexandra Popp bagged a brace in her side's opening win over Morocco but it was one of her goal celebrations that caught the eye – she pointed to the sky and pretended to be on the phone like iconic alien E.T.!

McCABE'S CORNER-KICK MAGIC!

Captain Katie McCabe scored Republic of Ireland's first-ever Women's WC goal from a corner after just four minutes against Canada! Sadly, Ireland were still knocked out in the group stage.

 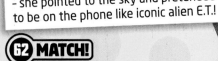

SPANISH STUNNER!

Talking about screamers, Spain's Teresa Abelleira drove in a stunning strike from distance to open the scoring against Zambia inside ten minutes! It opened the floodgates as the silky Spaniards went on to beat the African debutants 5-0!

MATILDAS MISERY!

Nigeria produced one of the shocks of the tournament after coming back from 1-0 down to beat Australia 3-2 – despite the hosts being 30 places above them in the world rankings and having 28 shots on goal!

GOAAAAAALAZOOOOOOOOOO!

Argentina's Sophia Braun scored one of the goals of the tournament against South Africa! She controlled a bouncing ball from way outside the area before sending a half-volley into the top bins. Epic tekkers!

LETHAL LAUREN!

Making her first-ever start in a major international tournament in England's match against Denmark, Lauren James picked up the ball outside the penalty area and curled in a screamer. And it was the winner!

CLASSY CAICEDO!

Colombia wonderkid Linda Caicedo produced a top piece of tekkers before curling a shot into the top corner v Germany to help her side pull off one of the greatest-ever Women's World Cup shocks!

ROMAN HAUG'S HAT-TRICK!

Sophie Roman Haug hit a hat-trick as former WWC champs Norway thrashed the Philippines 6-0 to reach the last 16 of the competition. Her third goal came in the fifth minute of stoppage-time so she left it really late!

WOMEN'S WORLD CUP 2023 Scrapbook!

BRUGTS BANGERS!

Netherlands smashed seven goals past Vietnam in their group-stage demolition, but the pick of the goals came from Esmee Brugts – she scored two almost identical long-range curling efforts!

WENDIE WITH THE WINNER!

Les Bleues captain Wendie Renard headed a late winner as France beat Brazil in a thrilling group-stage game between two WWC giants! Gaffer Herve Renard became the first manager to win a game at both the men's and women's World Cup!

FOUR-GOAL HAUL!

Former champions Japan stormed to a 4-0 victory over high-flying Spain to top Group C in what was one of the most effective team displays of the tournament!

THE JAMES SHOW!

The individual performance of the tournament came from Lauren James v China! She scored two absolute worldies – and had another ruled out – as well as grabbing a hat-trick of assists to become the first England player to be directly involved in five or more goals in a single WWC match!

HOLDERS DUMPED OUT!

After USA v Sweden went to penalties, US keeper Alyssa Naeher appeared to have saved Lina Hurtig's all-important effort at the second attempt but, after checking with the VAR, Sweden's goal was awarded to spark wild celebrations!

ROCKET SHOT!

Talking about penalties, Chloe Kelly's winning effort against Nigeria in the last 16 shootout was a thunderbolt – at 110.79 km/h, it became the fastest shot of the whole tournament. Whooooosh!

PENALTY PRESSURE!

Co-hosts Australia reached the WWC semi-finals for the first time as they beat France in a dramatic penalty shootout in Brisbane! Matildas goalkeeper Mackenzie Arnold was the star of the show as she made three all-important saves in the shootout!

COMEBACK QUEENS!

England keeper Mary Earps got caught out by a cheeky lob from Colombia midfielder Leicy Santos in the quarter-finals, but Sarina Wiegman's side showed spirit to earn a 2-1 win thanks to awesome goals by Lauren Hemp and Alessia Russo!

TEENAGE KICKS!

Teenage forward Salma Paralluelo came off the bench to score a 111th-minute winner for Spain – becoming the nation's youngest-ever WWC goalscorer – to beat the Netherlands and reach the WWC semi-finals for the first time!

LATE DRAMA!

The drama didn't stop there for Spain! Their semi-final with Sweden exploded into life in the final stages, with three goals in nine minutes – Olga Carmona scored a long-range winner just two minutes after Sweden's equaliser!

FIRST-TIME FINALISTS!

The Lionesses joined Spain in the final after a mega tense clash with co-hosts Australia, headlined by some incredible finishes! Ella Toone's drive was cancelled out by Sam Kerr's sick 25-yard stunner, before Hemp and Russo secured the W!

SPAIN WIN THEIR FIRST WOMEN'S WORLD CUP!

The final came down to a head-to-head between Spain and England and was won by La Roja after a first-half Carmona strike! Spain's Aitana Bonmati won the Golden Ball, while Japan's Hinata Miyazawa picked up the Golden Boot with five goals!

WOMEN'S SUPER LEAGUE RECORDS!

MATCH delves into the Women's Super League record books...

APPEARANCES

Rock-solid Tottenham defender Kerys Harrop played her 178th game in the competition in April 2023, breaking the record for the most WSL appearances of all time! The former Birmingham captain made her WSL debut back in 2011!

ASSISTS

Arsenal and England superstar Beth Mead is the only player in Women's Super League history to bag at least 40 assists in the competition! The majority have been at The Gunners, but she also got some at her first club Sunderland!

YOUNGEST SCORER

Four-time PFA Young Player of the Year award winner Lauren Hemp became the WSL's youngest-ever goalscorer when she netted for Bristol City aged just 16 years and 258 days old back in April 2017!

YOUNGEST PLAYER

By coming on as a sub against Everton in 2017, then-Arsenal winger Lauren James put her name in the record books by becoming the youngest player in Women's Super League history! She was just 16 years and 30 days old!

CLEAN SHEETS

No keeper has made more appearances in the WSL than Mary Earps, while she was also the first goalie to keep 50 clean sheets in the competition. She previously played for Birmingham before joining Man. United in 2020!

COACH WINS

The most successful manager in WSL history is Emma Hayes! As well as taking charge of the most matches, she's also overseen the most victories, lifted the most titles and won the most Manager of the Year awards!

VIVIANNE MIEDEMA

The Arsenal legend has loads of WSL records to her name!

ALL-TIME WSL TABLE!

These teams have the most all-time points...

1 **ARSENAL**
2 **CHELSEA**
3 **MAN. CITY**
4 **BIRMINGHAM**
5 **EVERTON**
6 **LIVERPOOL**
7 **MAN. UNITED**
8 **READING**
9 **BRISTOL CITY**
10 **WEST HAM**

Most goal contributions	112	Joint-most goals in a single season	22	Most hat-tricks	5	First player to score v every side she's faced	1
Most all-time goals	78	Most goals in a calendar month	10	Most assists in one game	4		
Quickest to reach 50 goals	50	Most goals in one game	6	Most hat-tricks in a single season	3		

Stats correct up to start of the 2023-24 season.

BIG MATCH QUIZ!

How many of these tough women's footy teasers can you get right?

SPOT THE BALL!

Mark where you think the ball is in this Women's Super League action pic!

BOGUS BADGE!

Name the Women's Championship club this cool badge belongs to!

BABY FACE

Name the Man. City Women's star in this snap from before they were famous!

NAME THE NATION!

What countries do these WSL ballers represent?

1. Khadija Shaw

2. Vivianne Miedema

3. Clare Wheeler

4. Lucia Garcia

5. Melanie Leupolz

6. Kenza Dali

ACE ACTIVITY

WORDSEARCH

Find 30 Women's Super League stars from the 2022-23 season in this giant grid!

Asseyi	Blundell	Eikeland	Ildhusoy	Lehmann	Smith
Bartrip	Coombs	Evans	James	Maanum	Spence
Bennison	Dali	Graham	Kelly	Pacheco	Toone
Blackstenius	Daly	Greenwood	Ladd	Shaw	Turner
Blindkilde	Earps	Hanson	Le Tissier	Shimizu	Zelem

```
Z T O F L J A A G F P G I I U I R N K C F Y N D V Z M C B T Z B
N O E N G F Q D P Y L V Q O T F W U S M D B R Q O J P X S U H L
N P T P L N Y P O S Q L H N F Z R Y A Q S Q N U R J J G O P P I
C P U J T Q C L M E Q Z I C X U R C P M U Y T K B W O U I Z K N
E D M V K N X V C O N P F C L O Z A K W E R Z S V C J J C S O D
Y M T K W G R W L T Z I J K L L E T I S S I E R W J Z G G F O K
T A E C K N B O R F B E K H V M T E F A T P A S R C O U F C U I
X M Z C M O T G O B F J M M O W C V S H G S N P K J J L E Y Y L
J V N E W C M O C L L Y N N N G A T Z Z X Y T S M E F H F G H D
P O L J F F O Z D U D L L F L O R S B Y F O T A P N C V V R S E
H E A I G K Q D T N R B F F K E H E H O V M K E D A Y K Z I X T
Z V P A X M A D T D S U S O N D H E U Z J F M P Q R C K Q S K
V P J D Q A W B O E U P R S N R Q M G N K S T G V Z S T D D E J
U C N S A S D H O L X B E T S S J K A D W N A O V U H H Q L I J
Z H N B J S L N N L K D B N K P I S J N D O P R T L I P S U K Y
Y J M Z E E M M E F T X J C C S S L M L N J O K S T M C M Q E J
G P G C B Y V T U R N E R J F E S O J H F Q Q D Q F I I I P L B
P V U K A I P E M X B T O A C O J Y D Z H C F N H O Z L T C A K
E K A S R I I D A L Y E C R S N N K R O C S L Y A R U D H J N X
A V O D T X Q H G B D L B Q P B T D P Z Y Q C L F L W H I A D I
I B Q X R Y P J B Y F C K G Q K Q G A Y W L K J T J U A K W M
J S L N I C L O A F I V Z Z I U S Z H X H D P B T P Y S L H X A
B H O H P X F K M C O R P T V K O S S L M G M U H R J O X A Q D
J A B M Z D V E E S J V P P J N E G K O X L J C I E O Y T N J C
D W S U H U D I S D K Y V N Y H S N F Z I W B S Q I O Z R S E X
B L A C K S T E N I U S K Q O V X Y M V G Y X O B D W C L O F B
E P B B C F Y D L T M M Y V V X X A Q Q V Z J C G E H F D O N V K
A M K I T I O M O T B E C F Z M Y U L N N I C G N E A R P S K E
R K U Y P M I A D R P B Q O T K J P Y I B I B K N B D L M E R X
A V R O A Y C A Y U O S D M O G T I K U L V G H I C A A E H Y O
O T R H Z K Y N V H L E J A F M B X L A U J S Q S Y P D P H N Z
T U A H K Z F U M U C K F A F B Y D P O F K O J Z D Q N Q G
C R T X H C I M G U V B B Q C V X S J H C F Y D N U N E C I K D
G M Q J Q C Q D F S M F H K E L L Y O X J X P E V A N S L X N X
```

ANSWERS ON PAGE 94

TOP 10
GOLD-MEDAL WINNERS

With the Olympics coming to Paris in 2024, we check out the best footy teams to win Gold!

URUGUAY MEN
AMSTERDAM 1928

The first World Cup wasn't held until 1930, so during the 1920s the Olympic Games was the way to decide the world's best team! Uruguay won back-to-back gold medals in 1924 and 1928, and then went on to lift the first-ever World Cup trophy on home soil two years later – what a team!

SPAIN MEN
BARCELONA 1992

This was the first time that football at the Olympics was an Under-23 tournament. Playing in his home city, a young Pep Guardiola was the star of the Spain side, scoring the first goal of the Games with a banging free-kick, and captaining the team to Gold on home soil!

NIGERIA MEN
ATLANTA 1996

No African team had ever won Gold at the football Olympics before Nigeria! They did it in style too - not only did their squad contain future Prem legends like Jay-Jay Okocha and Nwankwo Kanu, they won the semi-final v Brazil and final v Argentina with dramatic late goals!

USA WOMEN
ATLANTA 1996

While Nigeria were making history in the Men's Games, USA became the first-ever female champions! After women's football joined the Olympics, it was no surprise to see the hosts pick up Gold with a 2-1 win over China in the final!

CAMEROON MEN
SYDNEY 2000

After winning their first match 3-2 in a topsy-turvy clash against Kuwait, the drama never stopped for Cameroon! In the quarter-finals they beat a Brazil team starring Ronaldinho with a Golden Goal, came from 1-0 down in the last six minutes to sink Chile in the semis, and defeated Spain on penalties in the final!

NORWAY WOMEN
SYDNEY 2000

Norway were a major force in women's football in the 1980s and '90s, winning two European Championships and a World Cup in that time. Their last major honour came in Sydney in 2000 – they beat European champs Germany in the semis and reigning champs USA in the final!

ARGENTINA MEN
BEIJING 2008

When you look back at Argentina's 2008 squad, it's no surprise they won Gold! It was packed with top talent, including future national team skipper Javier Mascherano, Man. City legend Sergio Aguero, superstar winger Angel Di Maria and, the main man himself, Lionel Messi!

USA WOMEN
LONDON 2012

In the history of Olympic football, no other team has ever won three Gold medals in a row! Led by legends like Megan Rapinoe, Carli Lloyd and Alex Morgan, their win was made even sweeter by beating Japan in the final - a year after losing to them in the World Cup final!

CANADA WOMEN
TOKYO 2020

Canada legend Christine Sinclair holds the all-time record for most international goals, and won Bronze medals in both 2012 and 2016 before finally getting her hands on Gold in Japan in 2021 – an Olympics delayed by a year due to COVID. Canada beat rivals USA in the semis before seeing off Sweden on pens in the final!

BRAZIL MEN
TOKYO 2020

After winning both the 2016 and 2020 Games, Brazil will be chasing history in Paris in 2024. Last time round they were fired to Gold by Tottenham's Richarlison, who starred alongside other Prem stars Antony, Bruno Guimaraes and Diego Carlos to win Gold!

IS-TAT-YOU?

MATCH presents some of football's best and worst footy statues and gives them a rating out of 10!

BOBBY MOORE

Probably the GOAT footy statue, this brilliant Moore memorial outside Wembley Stadium really captures the character of England's 1966 World Cup-winning captain. Class!

10/10

MOHAMED SALAH

1/10

This has to go down as one of the weirdest footy statues in history! We have no idea why Mo Salah's arms are so small in relation to his body, or why his upper body is so long!

DIEGO MARADONA

6/10

The long hair, high shorts and World Cup trophy definitely give it away that this is the Argentina legend, but we think they let themselves down a little bit with the generic-looking face!

THIERRY HENRY

8/10

CELEBRATION CORNER

Arsenal unveiled this epic statue to celebrate the club's 125th anniversary! It captures their club record goalscorer's iconic knee-slide celebration after he scored a wondergoal against North London rivals Tottenham in 2002! It's a real favourite among Gunners fans!

FREDDIE LJUNGBERG MANCHESTER UTD MAY 2002

CHARLIE NICHOLAS v LIVERPOOL APRIL 1987

THIERRY HENRY v LEEDS JANUARY 2001

PATRICK VIEIRA v TOTTENHAM APRIL 2001

Fly Emirates

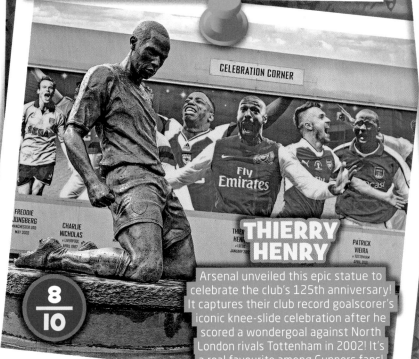

DAVID BECKHAM

This is a strong statue! As well as the cool action pose, the blur effect to his left arm makes it seem as if Beckham's bending a ball in front of your very eyes. Well fancy!

9/10

SERGIO AGUERO

To commemorate the iconic "Aguerooo" moment of the 2011-12 season, Man. City revealed this statue outside the Etihad Stadium! It's quite cool, but some critics reckon it looks more like Toni Kroos from side-on...

7/10

GEORGE BEST, DENIS LAW & SIR BOBBY CHARLTON

The simplistic statue of Man. United's "Holy Trinity" standing in arms, while looking towards the Old Trafford stadium, is one of the most iconic monuments in world football!

9/10

MICHAEL ESSIEN

We're still a little bit traumatised from the first time we saw this statue of the ex-Chelsea and Ghana international in 2018, but we guess it's the thought that counts...

3/10

MICHAEL JACKSON

We know, we know, Michael Jackson never graced the Craven Cottage pitch, nor wore the famous white jersey of Fulham, but we can't do a feature on statues and not mention this wacky one outside the West London ground!

3/10

CRISTIANO RONALDO

We reckon CR7 must have been fuming when this bonkers statue was revealed at Madeira airport on his home island! It kind of looks nothing like him!

2/10

CARTOON TIME!

Don't forget to add the Man. City badge to the shirt!

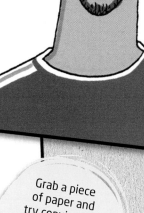

Grab a piece of paper and try copying the cartoon – you can use tracing paper if you find it easier!

For more cool Dreadfully Drawn designs, visit dreadfullydrawn.co.uk and follow him on social media @dreadfullydrawn

Have a go at drawing some of the other epic players on this page too!

Send your drawings into MATCH – by email **match.magazine@kelsey.co.uk** or social media – and we'll feature our faves in the mag. What are you waiting for?

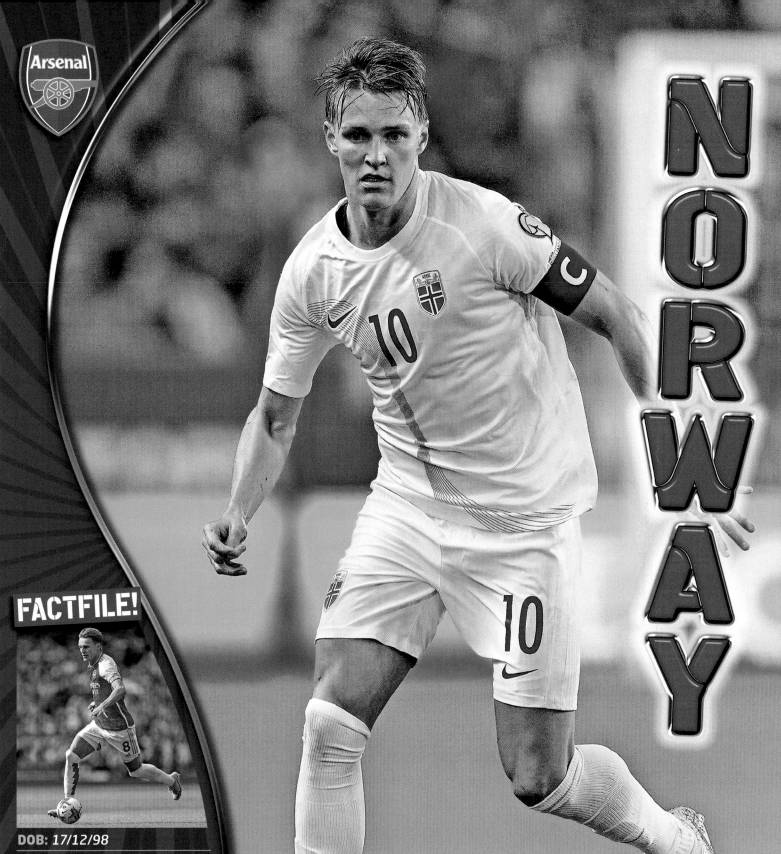

NORWAY

Arsenal

FACTFILE!

DOB: 17/12/98

Club: Arsenal

Country: Norway

Position: Att. midfielder

Top Skill: Close control

Footy Fact! Martin Odegaard was the youngest player ever to feature in a Euro qualifier when he came on as a sub against Bulgaria in 2014 aged just 15 years and 300 days!

ODEGAARD

JUDE BELLINGHAM

REAL MADRID'S MAGIC MAN!

FACTPACK

DOB: *29/06/03*
Club: *Real Madrid*
Country: *England*
Position: *Midfielder*
Boots: *adidas Predator*
Top Skill:
Elite game intelligence

SKILLS

Bellingham's got a sick first touch and loves to drive forward and make things happen every time he gets on the ball! His height and strength mean that he's almost impossible to knock off the ball once he gets going! The England man has world-class quality in his boots as well - whether he's picking out a pass or taking a shot, he's laser accurate!

STORY

Bellingham was the youngest player in Birmingham's history when he burst onto the scene for his boyhood club as a 16-year-old in 2019! Since then, he's racked up over £100 million in transfer fees from two of the biggest clubs in Europe – Dortmund snapped him up in 2020, and he was so good for the German giants that Real Madrid spent £88.5m on him last summer!

STYLE

What makes Bellingham so fun to watch is that he's a totally all-action player. When he was young, his coach asked him what type of midfielder he wanted to be - a DM that wears No.4, a box-to-box No.8 or an attacking No.10? Young Jude decided he wanted to be all three at once, and when you add those numbers up you get 22 – which was his shirt number at both Birmingham and Borussia Dortmund!

HE PLAYS LIKE...
Zinedine Zidane

Tall but skilful, creative but tough, and capable of producing magic with either foot, Bellingham is the perfect man to wear Zidane's famous No.5 shirt at Real Madrid!

WHAT'S IN STORE FOR 2024?

Jude has done unbelievably well in his young career so far, but things could get even better in 2024! Before the start of the season, his only major trophy was the German Cup with Dortmund in 2021 but he'll be targeting the La Liga and Champions League crowns with Real Madrid, and Euro 2024 with England!

SHOW REEL!

Take a look at some of Bellingham's best moments...

Birmingham v Stoke, 2019
Bellingham's first-ever goal took a lucky deflection on its way in, but made him his boyhood club's youngest-ever goalscorer!

Dortmund v Arminia Bielefeld, 2021
Bellingham's third Bundesliga goal came as he danced through the Bielefeld defence, before dinking the ball over the keeper!

Dortmund v Stuttgart, 2022
A brilliant turn, a great dribble and a beautiful finish curled into the bottom corner from the edge of the box!

England v Iran, 2022
By scoring England's first goal in Qatar, Bellingham became The Three Lions' second-youngest World Cup goalscorer!

England v Senegal, 2022
The midfielder was one of England's best performers in their last-16 victory, and capped his display with a classy assist!

The Premier League's 150 CLUB

In 2023, Tottenham superstar Heung-min Son became the 35th player to reach 150 goals and assists combined in the Premier League! Take a look at the other stars to hit that milestone...

35

Dion Dublin 151
111 GOALS & 40 ASSISTS

The tall striker scored Premier League goals for Man. United, Coventry and Aston Villa, while his flick-ons and link-up play helped him bag assists for his strike partners as well!

34

David Silva 153
60 GOALS & 93 ASSISTS

One of the best playmakers that the Prem has ever seen, Silva had X-ray vision and a magical left foot that helped him create chances out of nothing - that's why he's a Man. City legend!

33

Heung-Min Son 155*
103 GOALS & 52 ASSISTS

The South Korea captain notched his 100th Prem goal last April in a 2-1 win over Brighton - just weeks after bagging his 50th PL assist! He's the first-ever Asian player to reach both milestones!

32

Romelu Lukaku 156
121 GOALS & 35 ASSISTS

At his best, the Belgium beast was unstoppable for West Brom, Everton and Man. United! When he scored his 100th PL goal in 2018, he was the youngest foreign player to ever reach the landmark. Legend!

*Stats correct up to start of the 2023-24 season

31

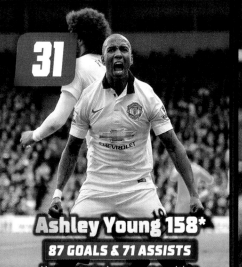

Ashley Young 158*

87 GOALS & 71 ASSISTS

Young started out as an exciting young talent at Watford and Aston Villa, became a super consistent winger at Man. United, then dropped back to full-back and re-joined Villa! Now at Everton, he's still one of the best crossers around!

30

Didier Drogba 159

104 GOALS & 55 ASSISTS

The first African player to score 100 Prem goals, Drog won two Golden Boots, including in 2009-10 when he scored a whopping 29 times! His partnership with Frank Lampard helped him pick up tons of goals and assists!

29

Cesc Fabregas 161

50 GOALS & 111 ASSISTS

Whether he was playing for Arsenal or Chelsea, the Spain star was always one of the most creative midfielders in the league! He also had an eye for goal, as he showed in 2009-10 when he notched a career-best 15 Prem goals!

28

Paul Scholes 162

107 GOALS & 55 ASSISTS

Before he retired, Scholes was a deep-lying midfielder that bossed games with his unreal passing range, but in his early years he bombed forward to score goals! Spectacular volleys were his speciality!

25=

Matt Le Tissier 163

100 GOALS & 63 ASSISTS

At times, Le Tissier single-handedly kept Southampton in the Premier League with his ability to score or create goals out of nothing! His 100th PL goal was also the last-ever goal at The Saints' old stadium, The Dell!

25=

Emile Heskey 163

110 GOALS & 53 ASSISTS

Heskey's strike partners absolutely loved playing with him because he worked hard and bullied defenders to help create space! The former England powerhouse scored for Leicester, Liverpool, Birmingham, Wigan and Aston Villa!

25=

Robbie Keane 163

126 GOALS & 37 ASSISTS

The Republic of Ireland's all-time record scorer bagged Premier League goals for six different clubs – Coventry, Leeds, Tottenham, Liverpool, West Ham and Aston Villa. Hero!

23=

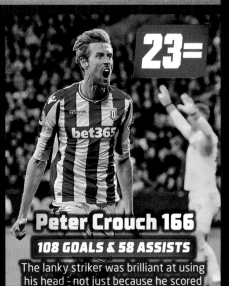

Peter Crouch 166

108 GOALS & 58 ASSISTS

The lanky striker was brilliant at using his head - not just because he scored more PL headers than any other player in history, but also because he was clever enough to create chances for his strike partners!

23=

Kevin De Bruyne 166*

64 GOALS & 102 ASSISTS

In April 2023, De Bruyne notched his 100th Prem assist in his 237th appearance, making him the fastest player to ever reach that milestone! By the time he leaves England, he'll definitely be much higher up this list!

21=

Dwight Yorke 173
123 GOALS & 50 ASSISTS

The Trinidad & Tobago legend made history in 2000 as the first foreign player to reach 100 Premier League goals! The year before, he starred in Man. United's treble-winning season, finishing as their top goalscorer in all comps and notching 11 PL assists!

20

Raheem Sterling 174*
115 GOALS & 59 ASSISTS

Only one winger has scored more Premier League goals than the England star, who has been a consistent PL performer for ten seasons now after bursting onto the scene as a thrilling teenager at Liverpool!

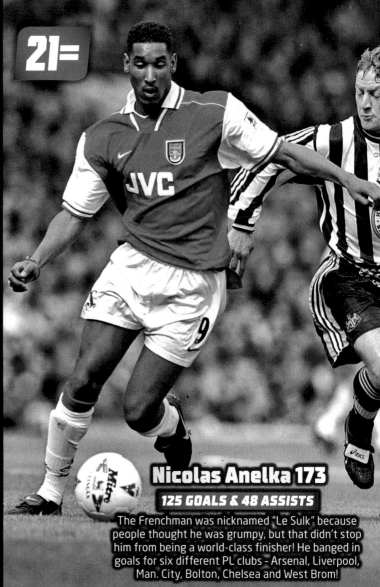

21=

Nicolas Anelka 173
125 GOALS & 48 ASSISTS

The Frenchman was nicknamed "Le Sulk" because people thought he was grumpy, but that didn't stop him from being a world-class finisher! He banged in goals for six different PL clubs - Arsenal, Liverpool, Man. City, Bolton, Chelsea and West Brom!

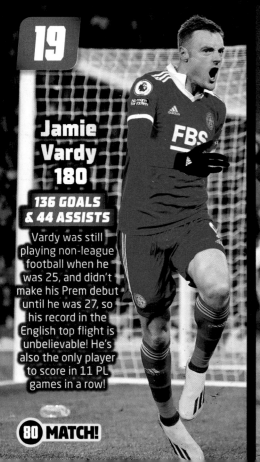

19

Jamie Vardy 180
136 GOALS & 44 ASSISTS

Vardy was still playing non-league football when he was 25, and didn't make his Prem debut until he was 27, so his record in the English top flight is unbelievable! He's also the only player to score in 11 PL games in a row!

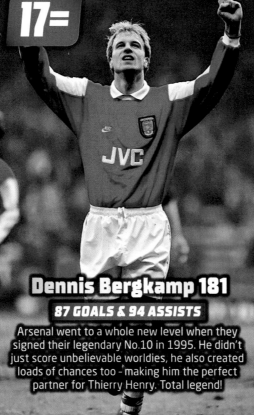

17=

Dennis Bergkamp 181
87 GOALS & 94 ASSISTS

Arsenal went to a whole new level when they signed their legendary No.10 in 1995. He didn't just score unbelievable worldies, he also created loads of chances too - making him the perfect partner for Thierry Henry. Total legend!

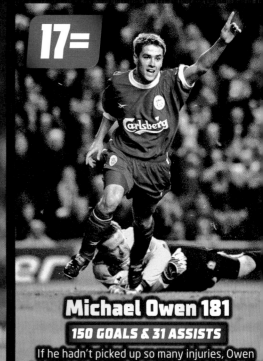

17=

Michael Owen 181
150 GOALS & 31 ASSISTS

If he hadn't picked up so many injuries, Owen would be much higher up this list! He burst onto the scene as a world-class wonderkid, and was only 23 when he scored his 100th PL goal - the youngest player to reach the milestone!

16

Jimmy Floyd Hasselbaink 185
127 GOALS & 58 ASSISTS

In 1998-99 while playing for Leeds, the explosive Dutch striker finished joint-top of both the Premier League's goal and assist charts! He later banged in goals for Chelsea, Middlesbrough and Charlton!

15

Jermain Defoe 195
162 GOALS & 33 ASSISTS

The ex-England striker is the only player in Prem history to score five goals in one half, when he destroyed Wigan's defence in Tottenham's 9-1 thrashing in 2009. Epic!

14

Robin van Persie 197
144 GOALS & 53 ASSISTS

RVP won back-to-back Prem Golden Boots in 2011-12 and 2012-13, first with Arsenal and then with Man. United. He's also the only player to score in nine consecutive away games in the Prem!

12=

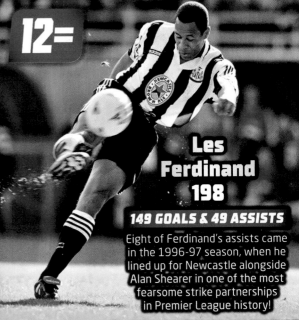

Les Ferdinand 198
149 GOALS & 49 ASSISTS

Eight of Ferdinand's assists came in the 1996-97 season, when he lined up for Newcastle alongside Alan Shearer in one of the most fearsome strike partnerships in Premier League history!

12=

Mohamed Salah 198*
139 GOALS & 59 ASSISTS

Salah has collected tons of records since arriving at Liverpool in 2017, and there are plenty more to come. It's only a matter of time until he passes 200 goals and assists combined!

11

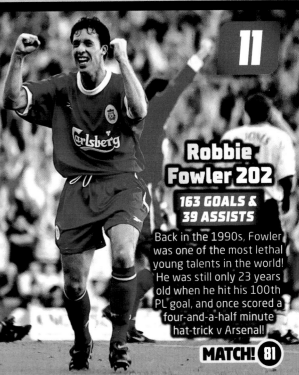

Robbie Fowler 202
163 GOALS & 39 ASSISTS

Back in the 1990s, Fowler was one of the most lethal young talents in the world! He was still only 23 years old when he hit his 100th PL goal, and once scored a four-and-a-half minute hat-trick v Arsenal!

10 Steven Gerrard 212

120 GOALS & 92 ASSISTS

Gerrard bagged loads of goals from midfield, and finished as Liverpool's top scorer in three different seasons, but he was at his best when he had a world-class striker like Fernando Torres or Luis Suarez ahead of him to create chances for!

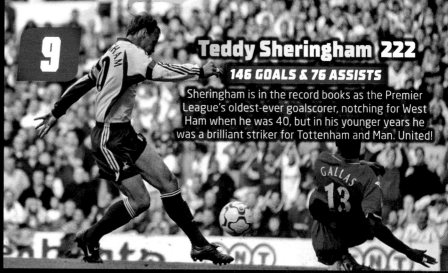

9 Teddy Sheringham 222

146 GOALS & 76 ASSISTS

Sheringham is in the record books as the Premier League's oldest-ever goalscorer, notching for West Ham when he was 40, but in his younger years he was a brilliant striker for Tottenham and Man. United!

8 Sergio Aguero 231

184 GOALS & 47 ASSISTS

Thanks partly to smashing home a record 12 Premier League hat-tricks, Aguero is the highest-scoring foreign player in PL history! If he'd spent his whole career in England, he'd probably be at the top of this list!

7 Thierry Henry 249

175 GOALS & 74 ASSISTS

During his peak years, Henry was the king of the Prem – he could destroy defences for fun! The France legend remains the only player to bag over 20 goals and 20 assists in the same season!

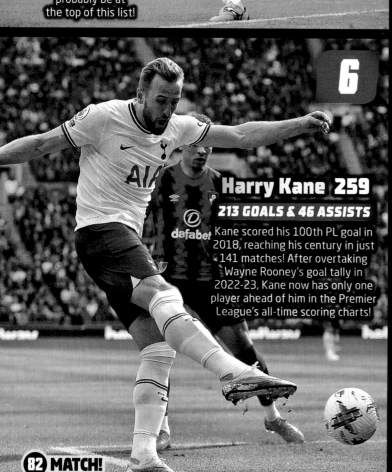

6 Harry Kane 259

213 GOALS & 46 ASSISTS

Kane scored his 100th PL goal in 2018, reaching his century in just 141 matches! After overtaking Wayne Rooney's goal tally in 2022-23, Kane now has only one player ahead of him in the Premier League's all-time scoring charts!

5 Andy Cole 260

187 GOALS & 73 ASSISTS

Cole was an absolute goal machine and one of the best finishers that English footy has ever seen – and his record is even more impressive when you remember that he didn't take penalties!

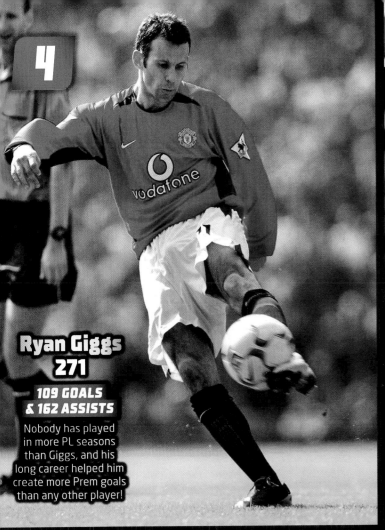

4

Ryan Giggs
271

**109 GOALS
& 162 ASSISTS**

Nobody has played in more PL seasons than Giggs, and his long career helped him create more Prem goals than any other player!

3

Frank Lampard
279

177 GOALS & 102 ASSISTS

Lampard is one of the best goalscoring midfielders of all time! He was deadly from penalties, had a rocket long-range shot and timed his runs into the box perfectly to get on the end of crosses and passes!

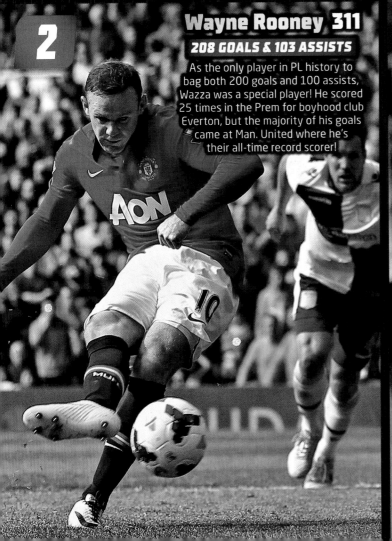

2

Wayne Rooney 311

208 GOALS & 103 ASSISTS

As the only player in PL history to bag both 200 goals and 100 assists, Wazza was a special player! He scored 25 times in the Prem for boyhood club Everton, but the majority of his goals came at Man. United where he's their all-time record scorer!

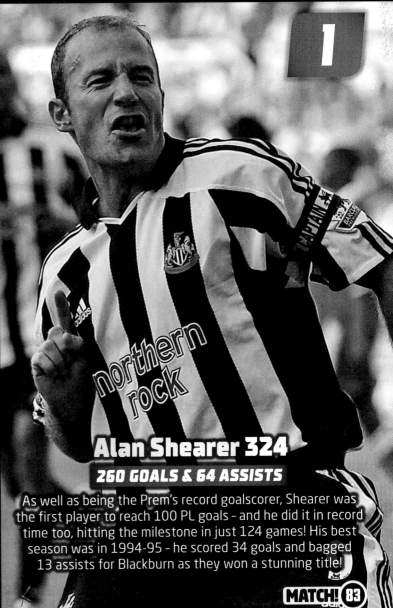

1

Alan Shearer 324

260 GOALS & 64 ASSISTS

As well as being the Prem's record goalscorer, Shearer was the first player to reach 100 PL goals - and he did it in record time too, hitting the milestone in just 124 games! His best season was in 1994-95 - he scored 34 goals and bagged 13 assists for Blackburn as they won a stunning title!

CRAZIEST

MATCH goes globetrotting to reveal some of the most bonkers team names in club football! Check this out...

FL FART
Vang. Norway

Yep, you read that right - there is a football club in Norway called Fart! The weird thing is, it's not the only Scandinavian club with a name that sounds like a trump - Middelfart, the hometown of Denmark and Man. United superstar Christian Eriksen, have a club in the Danish lower leagues too!

THE STRONGEST
La Paz. Bolivia

Originally known as "The Strong Football Club", they shortened their name a couple of years after being founded, and in 1930 lived up to it by winning the league title without conceding a single goal! That's more than can be said for Destroyers, who have never won the Bolivian league despite their name!

LIVERPOOL
Montevideo. Uruguay

Don't worry, Reds fans, your club hasn't moved to South America - there is a Liverpool in Uruguay too! Based in the capital city of Montevideo, they're not the only South American team with an English name - Everton de Vina del Mar play in Chile and Arsenal de Sarandi play in Argentina!

TEAM NAMES
in world football!

GRASSHOPPER CLUB ZURICH
Zurich, Switzerland

With 27 league titles and 19 Swiss Cups, Grasshopper are the most successful club in the history of Swiss football! They were founded in 1886 by an Englishman named Tom E. Griffith, but why did he name them after an insect? Nobody knows!

FC SANTA CLAUS
Rovaniemi, Finland

Although they play in the lower tiers of Finnish football, the Lapland-based side have one of the most famous names on the planet! The club's historians say that it was founded by Santa's elves having a kickaround during a break from wrapping presents!

MYSTERIOUS DWARFS
Cape Coast, Ghana

Cape Coast Mysterious Ebusua Dwarfs, to give them their full name, were one of the founding members of the Ghanaian Premier League! The African country is home to a whole load of weird and wacky team names. The Dwarfs' local rivals, for example, are called the Cape Coast Venomous Vipers!

WHO'S YOUR EFL TEAM?

ANSWER THESE TO FIND OUT!

Even if you already support a team in the English Football League, let's see who else you should be following...

1

2

WHICH TIER?

Does your team need to be playing in the Championship?

	If Yes, go to question 2!
	If No, go to question 4!

CLUB CREST!

Do you like football badges with animals on them?

	If Yes, go to question 3!
	If No, go to question 7!

3

LOFTUS ROAD W.12

LONDON BOROUGH OF HAMMERSMITH

LOCATION?

Do you want your team to be based in or around London?

	If Yes, go to question 5!
	If No, go to question 8!

PREM PAST?

Do you want to have a history of playing in the Premier League?

	If Yes, go to question 6!
	If No, go to question 9!

4

5

FAVOURITE COLOUR?

Is yellow one of your favourite colours?

✓	If Yes, you should support Watford!
✗	If No, you should support Millwall!

6

BEACH DAYS?

Do you want your team to be based near the coast?

✓	If Yes, you should support Portsmouth!
✗	If No, you should support Bradford!

7

RIVAL CLASHES!

Are games against local rivals one of your highlights of the season?

✓	If Yes, you should support Birmingham!
✗	If No, you should support Plymouth!

FAMOUS FAN?

Do you enjoy listening to Ed Sheeran's music?

✓	If Yes, you should support Ipswich!
✗	If No, you should support Norwich!

8

9

CELEBRITY OWNERS?

Do you want your club to have mega famous owners?

✓	If Yes, you should support Wrexham!
✗	If No, go to question 10!

10

STADIUM SIZE!

Do you prefer to have the largest stadium or the most compact?

✓	If the largest, you should support MK Dons!
✗	If the most compact, you should support Harrogate!

KAORU MITOMA

THE PROFESSOR OF DRIBBLING!

FACTPACK

DOB: 20/05/97
Club: Brighton
Country: Japan
Position: Winger
Boots: Puma Ultra
Top Skill: Demon dribbling

SKILLS

Everybody knows that dribbling is Mitoma's speciality - only four players completed more dribbles in the 2022-23 Prem season! The Japan superstar has endless energy, so he chases every ball and never stops running at his marker! He's also one of the bravest players around - he always wants the ball, and is not afraid of making mistakes!

STORY

It's common knowledge now, but before he turned pro Mitoma went to university and wrote a thesis all about dribbling! After graduating, he joined Japanese club Kawasaki Frontale and that's where Brighton spotted his top talent – they signed him in 2021 then loaned him out to Belgian club Union Saint-Gilloise. His breakout season came in 2022-23, when he showed his quality in the Prem and the World Cup. Legend!

STYLE

The key to Mitoma's dribbling ability is taking lots of small touches with the outside of his foot, waiting for his marker to make a move, then springing past them while they're off-balance! Defenders might know what he's trying to do, but that doesn't mean they can do anything to stop him! His special move is to burn down the left wing and cut the ball back for a forward to get an easy tap-in!

HE PLAYS LIKE...

Riyad Mahrez

Mahrez is a left-footed right-winger and Mitoma is a right-footer that cuts in from the left, but they're both tricky dribblers that terrorise full-backs! Plus, they were both absolute bargains when they arrived in the Prem!

WHAT'S IN STORE FOR 2024?

The 2023-24 campaign is a big one for Brighton as they compete in the Europa League for the first time in their history! Mitoma grabbed ten goals and seven assists in all competitions last season, but he'll need to chip in with much more if The Seagulls are going to kick on in the league and in Europe. In January, he'll be back in Qatar playing for Japan in the 2023 Asian Cup!

THE BEST GOALS THAT WEREN'T!

GRRR!!

MATCH revisits some of the greatest goals that either weren't given or didn't count!

▶ FRANK LAMPARD
GERMANY v ENGLAND, 2010

England were 2-1 down in their World Cup last 16 tie with Germany when they thought they'd equalised through a looping Frank Lampard effort. The ball floated over Manuel Neuer, struck the bar and clearly crossed the line, but the officials missed it - and The Three Lions went on to lose 4-1!

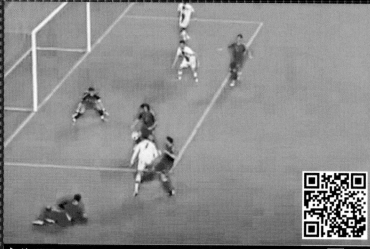

▶ CRISTIANO RONALDO
PORTUGAL v SPAIN, 2010

Ronaldo sat Spain's Gerard Pique on his backside with a savage piece of skill and then scooped the ball over Iker Casillas' head with the outside of his foot, only for his offside team-mate Nani to head the ball into the net on the line when it was already going in! Cue an on-pitch Ronaldo tantrum!

▶ KYLIAN MBAPPE
PSG v REAL MADRID, 2022

After being sent through on goal by PSG team-mate Neymar, Mbappe fooled one of the best goalkeepers in the world, Thibaut Courtois, with one of the most outrageous dummies you will ever see, before slotting the ball into an empty net! It was clearly offside, but it's still one of footy's biggest tragedies that it was ruled out!

▶ YOURI TIELEMANS
LEEDS v LEICESTER, 2023

The Belgium midfielder has scored some proper scorchers during his career, but he was denied one of his best in 2022-23! After the ball was rolled back to him outside the penalty area, he struck the sweetest possible shot with his laces that thundered into the top corner, only for it to be disallowed for an offside in the build-up!

▶ VADAINE OLIVER
CARLISLE v CREWE, 2013

Oliver scored a sick overhead-kick for Crewe at Carlisle, before realising the ref had stopped the match a second earlier for an injury to one of his team-mates! Once you've watched this clip, look up Dani Osvaldo's disallowed goal for Roma v Lecce for another acrobatic effort that was ruled out - this time incorrectly for offside!

AUSSTTRALIIA

KERR

FACTFILE!

DOB: 10/09/93

Club: Chelsea

Country: Australia

Position: Striker

Top Skill: Finishing

Footy Fact! Unstoppable goal grabber Sam Kerr is the highest scorer in Australia's history, overtaking Socceroos legend Tim Cahill's record in three fewer games. Wow!

LOVE MATCH?
GET IT DELIVERED EVERY FORTNIGHT!

PACKED EVERY ISSUE WITH....

MASSIVE STARS

RED-HOT GEAR

ACE INTERVIEWS

EPIC FEATURES

WEST HAM
AMAZING POSTERS

TIPS & QUIZZES!

SUBSCRIBE TO MATCH!...

CALL
01959 543 747
QUOTE: MATAN24

ONLINE
SHOP.KELSEY.
CO.UK/MATAN24

QUIZ ANSWERS!

Premier League Quiz — Pages 24–25

Flip For It: 1. Villarreal; 2. Black; 3. Newcastle; 4. Rodrigo; 5. Arsene Wenger; 6. Seven.

Higher or Lower?: 1. Lower; 2. Higher; 3. Higher; 4. Lower; 5. Lower.

Barmy Barnet: Andreas Pereira.

Legendary: 1. Man. United; 2. Leeds; 3. Arsenal; 4. Aston Villa; 5. Chelsea; 6. Everton.

Crossword: See below.

Euro Leagues Quiz — Pages 34–35

Napoli Quiz: 1. 1990; 2. True; 3. Georgia; 4. The Little Donkeys; 5. Victor Osimhen; 6. True.

Close-Up: 1. Vinicius Junior; 2. Gavi; 3. Jules Kounde; 4. Rodrygo.

Crazy Kit: Juventus.

Odd One Out: Lyon.

Footy Mis-Match: See top right.

EFL Quiz — Pages 52–53

Footy Maze: C – see right.

Player Battles: 1. Chuba Akpom; 2. Joel Piroe; 3. Carlton Morris; 4. Nathan Tella; 5. Oscar Estupinan.

Rhyme Time: 1. Teemu Pukki; 2. Jerry Yates; 3. Tom Ince; 4. Scott Hogan; 4. Will Keane; 5. Jack Clarke.

Kit Clash: Ken Sema.

Wordfit: See right.

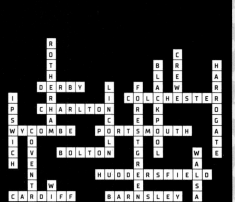

Women's Footy Quiz — Pages 68–69

Spot The Ball: 3 - See above.

Bogus Badge: London City Lionesses.

Baby Face: Lauren Hemp.

Name The Nation: 1. Jamaica; 2. Netherlands; 3. Australia; 4. Spain; 5. Germany; 6. France.

Wordsearch: See below.

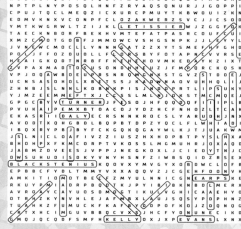

One point for each correct answer!

MY SCORE /131